LOST AT SEA

GREAT SHIPWRECKS OF HISTORY

Ronald Pearsall

SMITHMARK

This edition published in 1996 by
SMITHMARK Publishers,
a division of U.S. Media Holdings, Inc.,
16 East 32nd Street, New York, NY 10016

SMITHMARK books are available for bulk purchase for sales promotion and premium use.
For details write or call the manager of special sales,
SMITHMARK Publishers,
16 East 32nd Street,
New York, NY 10016;
(212) 532-6600.

This book was designed and produced by
Todtri Productions Limited
P.O. Box 572,
New York, NY 10116–0572
FAX: (212) 279–1241

Printed and bound in Singapore

Library of Congress Catalog Card Number 95–072460
ISBN 0–8317–7578–5

Author: Ronald Pearsall

Publisher: Robert Tod
Book Designer: Mark Weinberg
Production Coordinator: Heather Weigel
Senior Editor: Nicolas Wright
Project Editors: Edward Douglas, Cynthia Sternau
Assistant Editor: Don Kennison
Typesetting: Command-O, NYC

PICTURE CREDITS

CONTENTS

INTRODUCTION

The myriad treasures hidden in sunken wrecks beneath the ocean have inflamed human passions and imagination since the first sea voyages of ancient times. For centuries, only sunken ships resting near the surface or those smashed upon the shore could be easily explored. Though many tried to plumb the mysteries of the ocean, deep-sea diving was almost impossible. Today, there is almost no limit to marine exploration. The recent discovery of the wreck of the *Titanic* two-and-a-half miles below the surface is ample proof of a fully operative and long overdue technology for deep-sea research and salvage.

Shipwrecks are true time capsules filled with untold and intriguing treasures. Bounty hunters wish for a potential source of long-lost gold, silver, or diamonds, while scholars and historians hope for the mysteries of past ages to be suddenly revealed before their eyes.

The world has always been eager to explore the well-kept secrets of the deep, and the first successful diving machine, invented in 1531, was the diving bell. Early diving bells retained air for the diver to breath in an upper part of the apparatus, but after awhile the atmosphere would become unbreathable and need to be replenished. In 1717, astronomer Edmund Halley—who predicted the return of the comet which now bears his name—adapted the device by sending down barrels of air from which the diver breathed through a tube.

Leather diving suits with brass helmets were introduced around 1750, and, in one form or another, this uncomfortable and restricting equipment remained in use until recent times. Free diving equipment—diving suits without tubes to the surface—dates from the middle of the nineteenth century with the technological breakthrough of compressed air supplied in metal cylinders. Much of the development of SCUBA, the acronym for self-contained underwater breathing apparatus, took place in France. The first fully automatic aqualung appeared in 1939, and Otis Barton's bathysphere—a globular steel structure built to withstand enormous pressure—was also used in undersea exploration in the 1930s. Now, in the age of the miniature submarine, long-standing wrecks have become accessible for the first time, opening complex legal and ethical dilemmas in a new frontier of exploration.

Shipwrecks occur for many reasons—collisions, explosions, poor navigation, bad ship design, human error, incompetence, and sometimes just plain old-fashioned bad luck. Can maritime disasters be prevented? Ultimately, the answer must be that the sea is a dangerous and unpredictable natural element, and should be treated with great respect. The shipwrecks depicted in this book reveal through both image and text the dire consequences of these disasters as well as the formidable power of nature over men at sea.

RIGHT: Color print from *Le Petite Journal* (a French newspaper published on April 28, 1912) illustrating the sinking of the *Titanic*, the "ship God Himself could not sink." This print, however, shows the *Titanic* hitting an iceberg head-on, which is inaccurate, as it was a glancing blow to her side which ultimately felled the "unsinkable ship."

CHAPTER ONE

EARLY VOYAGERS
THE ANCIENT WORLD

The first powerful maritime nations in the ancient world were Egypt and Phoenicia. The earliest representations of Egyptian vessels date to 3000 B.C., and from these images it is known that there were as many as twenty-six oarsmen to a ship, plus a sail—usually one, though a foresail was sometimes added. Such a vessel was easily capable of carrying a full load of cattle, one of the main cargoes of that time. The Phoenicians occupied the coastal areas of what is now Syria and Lebanon, and were at their peak as a civilization from 1200 to 600 B.C. The earliest recorded Phoenician ships were biremes, vessels with two banks of oars staggered one above the other so that the oarsmen could row without getting in each others' way. Ship timbers were first tied together, and, in later innovations, pegged or jointed. The intrepid Phoenicians influenced the structure of the sea-going vessel for hundreds of years, and it is believed that they successfully circumnavigated Africa.

BELOW: Much of the internal trade in dynastic Egypt took place on the Nile, where vessels could have a shallow draft and did not need to be built as sturdily as ocean-going ships.

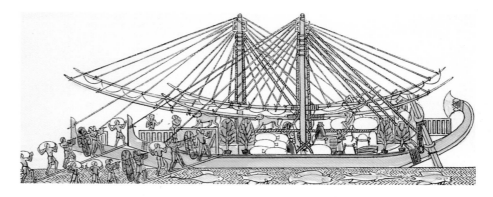

LEFT: Sailors, merchants, and travelers go about their business in a bustling seaport of ancient Phoenicia, about 1000 B.C.

FAR LEFT: Cleopatra, Queen of Egypt, on her royal ship at the battle of Actium, before her own fleet retreated at the sight of Octavian's forces.

FOLLOWING PAGE: This wooden model of an Egyptian supply ship of the 12th Dynasty (2500–1785 B.C.) shows the captain haranguing his crew of Canaanites.

ABOVE: An unusual arrangement of oars and a very elaborate rigging is evident in this model of a small Egyptian ship.

Greece

Gradually the number of oarsmen rose to sixteen banks. (One vessel had forty banks, but that was unusual.) Using oars for propulsion meant that the size of a ship had to remain relatively small—no more than 250 feet at the largest—for the bigger the ship was, the greater the effort needed to move it. By the time Greek civilization emerged as a sea-faring power in the fifth century B.C., boats were carrying crews of up to 120 men. Though none of these vessels exist today, we know of them through paintings on classic Greek vases.

Sea warfare was fast becoming sophisticated. Long, slim ships were built for speed and fighting (round ships were constructed for cargo), and the techniques of warfare were numerous and diverse. The ship itself, with a strengthened bow, was used as a battering ram. Weights were dropped on the enemy using long poles, burning arrows were shot, combustible material called Greek fire (which could burn underwater) was discharged from metal containers, and enemy ships were boarded by soldiers carried on the attacking vessel. Only boats powered by oars could be used as rams, since a sailing ship was ineffective unless driven head-on by a good breeze. Boarding and close man-to-man fighting was the most effective naval tactic in this era, for long-range battle was impossible until the advent of artillery in the fourteenth century.

BELOW: A model of a typical sixth-century B.C. Greek ship with oars and sails. This type of vessel was steered by an oar to the aft rather than a rudder.

RIGHT: The Greek trireme, a short ship propelled by multiple banks of oars, was built in tiers to accommodate as many rowers as possible.

RIGHT: An effective way of waging war at sea was to throw Greek fire at enemy ships. This highly combustible material, which even burned underwater, is believed to have consisted of sulfur, naptha, and quicklime.

RIGHT: This bronze head of a man, dating from the third to sixth centuries B.C., was among the more spectacular recoveries at the 1992 Brindisi excavation.

The Roman Empire

The naval presence of the Roman Empire (27 B.C.–A.D. 284) was a force to be reckoned with in both fighting strength and expansionist philosophy. Some Roman ships had turrets from which men with immensely long sickles cut down their opponents' sails, rendering the enemy ships useless. The Romans were organized; their enemies often were not. Sails were sometimes lowered in battle, or even left ashore when a battle was imminent. Sea battles were short-term, as ships had no space to carry the extra provisions for crew and warriors required for longer periods of warfare.

In 31 B.C., one of the most significant sea battles of the ancient world occurred at Actium, off the northwestern shore of Greece in the Ionion Sea. In a play for power that ultimately determined the success of the Roman Empire, Octavian, Julius Caesar's grand-nephew and heir, declared war against Marc Antony, an equal member of the ruling Triumvirate who had allied himself by marriage with Queen Cleopatra of Egypt. Each side held equally matched forces of four to five hundred ships and crews of more than one hundred thousand men. World history might have been written differently

BELOW: The prow of a typical Roman galley, similar to the ship which carried Marc Antony as he deserted his own navy at the battle of Actium in 31 B.C. to follow the fleeing Cleopatra back to Egypt.

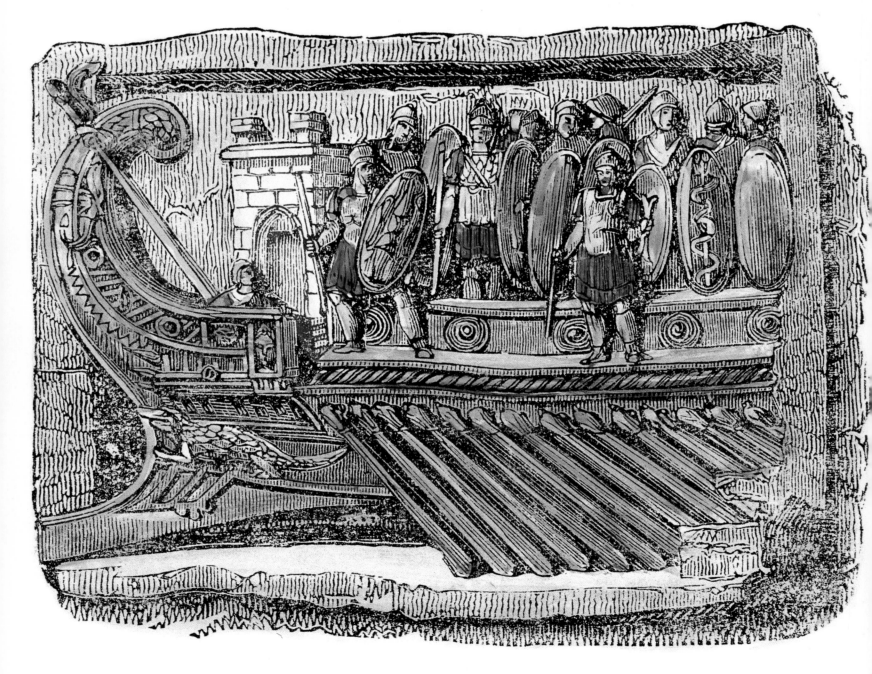

ABOVE: The far-ranging ships of the Roman Empire were not only mighty warships but also carried goods and colonists to distant ports as far away as Britain.

LEFT: A Roman ship is attacked by Macedonian pirates in 20 A.D., in a reconstruction taken from the classic silent film *Ben Hur* (1927).

had not three of Antony's six naval squadrons deserted at a critical point in battle. Watching from afar, Cleopatra made the decision to retreat with her own ships, and after Antony followed her, his own demoralized and leaderless fleet was captured or destroyed within a week. From this point forward there was no stopping Roman dominance on land and sea.

Ancient Wrecks

The Mediterranean Sea, where much of the trade and warfare of classical antiquity occurred, is a fairly shallow body of water. Laws regulating divers seeking sunken treasure are found in Greece as early as the third century B.C., yet from the earliest times, treasure hunters and scavengers plundered sunken and grounded vessels to which they had access, killing any survivors without mercy. As the ships were almost wholly built of wood, sometimes with lead sheathing, even those which escaped these predators have almost entirely disintegrated today.

But there are exceptions, often found by chance. One of the most interesting ancient wrecks ever discovered, an Etruscan vessel dating from about 600 B.C., lies off the small island of Giglio on the west coast of Italy, north of Rome. Thanks to the concern of the Italian government, the ship was given the status of a protected reserve, although whether that has impeded bounty hunters is another matter entirely.

The wreck at Giglio was discovered in 1961 at a depth of 150 feet, too far down for the old-time treasure hunters to touch. The man who found this ship tried to interest the local authorities in starting a museum, but he had no success. For a while there was a free-for-all with a good deal of souvenir hunting, and then the discovery was forgotten.

Later, in a search organized and funded by Oxford University from 1982 to 1986, many of the artifacts taken were tracked down and a new effort was made to find the wreck. Partway through the expedition, bounty hunters using an airlift (which sucks objects to the surface) significantly hampered the progress of the marine archaeologists at the site. Hundreds of artifacts, including two complete painted Greek vases, were lost. All of the "officially recovered" objects were placed in the Museum of Archaeology in Florence. Many had been preserved because they were encased in pitch—which was used to waterproof the ship or was perhaps a commercial cargo. The most spectacular find was a bronze helmet, cast in one piece and incised with fine representations of boars and snakes.

Marine Archaeology

One of the most fascinating features of marine archaeology is that the detective work is often as interesting as the find itself, especially when the recovered ship has rotted away and only the cargo or personal effects of the crew survive. The oldest wreck ever found dates from about 2500 B.C., and was discovered in 1975 off the island of Hydra

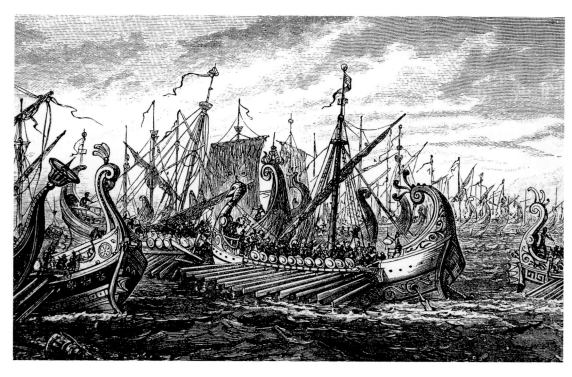

ABOVE: Among the techniques of ancient naval warfare was ramming, where the ship itself, with a strengthened bow, was used as a battering ram, as in this illustration of Greek ships ramming Persian vessels at the battle of Salamis in 480 B.C.

LEFT: Vases recovered from ancient wrecks often depict scenes from classical mythology. This Etruscan vase illustrates the story of Odysseus and the Sirens from Homer's *Odyssey*.

in Greece. It was lying in sixty-five feet of water in an area where twenty other ancient boats had been located, and was carrying a load of cooking pots, jugs, and cups, including a curious type of sauce boat. A twentieth of the ship's timber had survived—an unusually high proportion—which enabled an educated guess to be made about the ship's appearance.

In 1957 a wreck was discovered near Bodrum, Turkey, that dated back to about 1400 B.C. The waters there were treacherous, with sharp rocks rising to within six feet of the surface, and there were other sunken vessels also discovered at the site. Among the cargo recovered were bronze tools, broken amphoras (containers for wine or oil), and copper ingots, undoubtedly from Cyprus, a main source of copper. There were also Syrian scarabs inscribed with hieroglyphics.

Another rich find was made in a wreck recovered off Kyrenia, Cyprus. This ship, apparently pillaged at an earlier time, contained lead ingots, silver, and bronze statues. There were dining utensils, four hundred amphoras of different types, millstones, and almonds, later carbon-dated at about 370 B.C. More than half the hull had remained intact and was subsequently lifted from the sea. Another ship with an almost identical cargo was discovered in 1957 at a nearby site. She was estimated to be forty-seven feet long and fourteen feet in the beam, carrying a crew of four and weighing fourteen tons, of which half was cargo.

The remains of two ships dating from about 200 B.C. were discovered off Marseilles in 1953. Their cargo was large—eight thousand amphoras and no less than twelve thousand pieces of pottery—and this major expedition was the first to use underwater television to record its extraordinary finds. A more unusual discovery was made in the 1930s when a lake was drained near Rome, revealing pleasure barges believed to have belonged to the Emperor Caligula (A.D. 37–41).

Somewhere between the third and sixth centuries A.D., a cargo ship was downed in a storm in the Adriatic Sea near Brindisi. In 1992, a diver working only fifty feet deep saw what appeared to be a human foot protruding from the sea floor. This startling find led to the recovery of an extraordinary collection of bronze statues buried in the ancient wreck. The Brindisi bronzes, as they were subsequently called, were part of a shipment of worn and used statuary bound for a coastal foundry where it is thought they were to be recycled into armor or mirrors. But for scholars today, these beautiful fragments of sea-worn bronze, a material which lasts far longer in water than does marble, offer an unprecedented glimpse into lost details of ancient history and art.

Merchants and Warriors

Many of the wrecks discovered in the Mediterranean contained blocks of marble or marble statuary, for merchant ships, sometimes hardly more than small boats, were far more common than war vessels. Thus there was great excitement when a hundred-foot warship, built of several different kinds of wood, including maple and oak, was discovered off the coast of Sicily in the 1970s. The classical warship, though longer and sleeker than a cargo ship, needed to be fairly short in length so that the rowers could keep up a good speed (perhaps six knots was the average). It carried a large complement of men, both for rowing and for boarding during battle. The success of ramming or boarding depended on the skill of the oarsmen, and the Greeks developed their own special tactics, such as shaving off the oars of the opponent, the equivalent to the dismasting of the sail of a ship.

ABOVE: After defeating Genoa in 1380, Venice was unsurpassed among the great European sea-powers. This early Venetian warship is probably from about 1472, as the soldiers are bearing firearms.

LEFT: One of the many statues recovered in 1992 from a wreck near Brindisi in the Adriatic Sea. The vessel was believed to have been bound for a local foundry with a cargo of used statuary to be melted down into mirrors.

The Greeks used their naval prowess to full advantage during the battle of Salamis in 480 B.C., when Themistocles lead them in a decisive victory over the great Persian fleet assembled by Xerxes. One of the critical battles of the Persian War, this engagement took place in a narrow strait blockaded at the east and west end by the Persians, but when they tried to enter the strait their own overpowering strength proved their undoing, and the Persians were thrown into confusion. The Greeks seized exactly the right time to counterattack, and the Persians retreated in disarray, losing two hundred vessels as well as an army they had landed on an islet in the channel. The Greeks lost only forty ships out of a total of three hundred.

The ancient tactics of naval warfare changed little through the ages. If armies were fighting the last war but one, navies were fighting the last war but ten. Even in the age of artillery, when oarsmen were no longer used, the Spaniards made boarding a ship their main objective in battle. The gun was situated at the bow and only fired at the last minute, a near adaptation of the ramming tactics of ancient times. Battles were fought line abreast for many centuries; originally this formation was used to make the best use of ramming. In later years, inferior naval forces were tied together side by side to prevent boarding and were fortified with a barrier made of oars and spars. This tactic rarely worked, as the ships were then attacked from the flank.

In the Middle Ages ships were bearded—fortified with iron bands around the bow—both to ram and to resist ramming. This was the beginning of the development of plate armor, which would later cause ship designers to believe that their vessels were invincible.

Early Explorers and Colonists

When Mediterranean vessels ventured outside their home territory they had new problems to face, and if they were traders, extra provisions had to be taken on for the crew. It is likely that they sailed close to the coast. In contrast, the Vikings of northern Europe were fearless, sturdy, and strong. They used a combination of oars and sails, and were more adventurous in both spirit and technology. The Vikings had several types of boat, some with thirty oars, others with sixty-four oars and a crew of 240 men, and the so-called dragon boats which are believed to be depicted in the Bayeux Tapestry.

In 1880, a Viking ship was discovered in a tomb-mound in Norway; it was seventy-eight feet long, with a beam of sixteen feet, seven inches and a depth of five feet, nine inches. It had a high stem and stern, and was oak and clinker built, with sixteen oars on each side. This was the type of ship which ruled the northern seas and could even cross the Atlantic, for there is no doubt that the Vikings reached Newfoundland in the New World. Significant remains of their attempts to settle these areas have been recorded; eventually, however, the Vikings were repelled by the native Americans.

A number of wrecks from classical times have been discovered around the coasts of Britain, a colonial territory for many of the civilizations of the ancient world. The first Roman ship to be properly excavated was recovered near London's Westminster Bridge in 1910. Sixty- to seventy-feet long, it had apparently sunk at its moorings. In

RIGHT: The intrepid and adventurous Vikings discovered America long before Christopher Columbus, but although they reached Newfoundland, they did not settle there permanently.

both 1946 and 1963, Bronze Age vessels from about 1500 B.C., consisting of planks tied together sideways, were discovered on the bed of the River Humber in northern England. In 1962, in Blackfriars, London, the remains of a fifty-five-foot-long Romano-British flat-bottomed ship with a cargo of building stone was discovered. It was provisionally dated at A.D. 100–200.

With the rise of Byzantium and Venice and the gradual introduction of the galley—a new kind of fighting ship with one or two banks of oars—Rome gradually lost her hold in the Mediterranean. In A.D. 897, Alfred the Great, king of the West Saxons, defeated an invasion by a Danish fleet of three hundred sailing ships with a mere ten galleys. This early type of galley was superseded by the medieval man-of-war, a vessel with one bank of huge oars up to fifty feet in length, each oar rowed by up to seven men. So powerful was this design that for centuries the galley served as the ultimate fighting ship, and even the Spanish Armada included galleys as part of its invasion force.

The Crusades

The time of the Crusades was a great era for shipbuilders. King Richard I of England (1189–1199) built up a mixed fleet of 110 ships, which sailed from Dartmouth to Palestine in 1190. This force had increased to 230 vessels by the time

LEFT: A plundering expedition by the Vikings, who were known to be exceptionally cruel and rapacious on their raids.

LEFT: English warships of the fourteenth century, shortly before the invention of gunpowder revolutionized naval warfare.

RIGHT: The *White Ship* went down in 1120, drowning Prince William, the successor to the English throne. William distributed three casks of wine to the crew prior to sailing, and the ship subsequently foundered on rocks off the coast of France.

he arrived at his destination, an altercation with the Saracen fleet. One of the many ships destroyed by his galleys was an enormous three-masted ship containing 1,500 of the enemy.

Naval history was repeated in 1571 when the Holy League, an alliance of Spain, Venice, Genoa, and the Papal States fought an Ottoman Turkish fleet at the Battle of Lepanto (now the Gulf of Corinth). Heavy casualties were sustained on both sides, but the Holy League was victorious, capturing more than a hundred galleys and freeing thousands of Christian slaves. Though the Turkish navy was virtually destroyed, the Ottoman Empire was unimpaired and would remain so until the nationalist unrest of the nineteenth century.

The Crusades gave the British a taste for discovery and looting, breeding an antipathy toward other European nations with the same motive, and encouraging innovation in ship making and seamanship. Steering had previously been performed mainly by side-paddles; now a single rudder on the stern gradually became the preferred form, as it still is today. Ships still had forecastles and sterncastles, just as they did in Roman times. But the greatest spur to change in ship design and tactics was the discovery of gunpowder in the fourteenth century. At first guns were mounted on deck, but it was later realized that they needed protection, and artillery was brought below and fired through portholes. The standard naval bat-

ABOVE: Andrea Michieli's painting *The Battle of Lepanto*, which hangs in the Ducal Palace at Venice, captures the spirit of this great sea battle, the first major defeat of Turkey by the Christian powers.

tle formation changed from line abreast to line astern and remained unaltered until World War I.

In the north there was more interest in commerce than fighting, especially in long-distance commerce. Sweden, Denmark, and Norway built very large ships capable of carrying considerable amounts of cargo. Their navies, though capable, were of secondary importance.

Further south, however, war was never far away. The first of the true battleships arrived some time around 1370. As navigation and sailing techniques evolved, ships ventured further away from land, and sails became larger and more complicated with an immense amount of rigging. The fleet of England's Henry V (1413–1422) had vessels of nearly a thousand tons, though most were between 420 and 520 tons; these were regarded at the time as extraordinary war weapons. Sea battles between Britain and various European nations were numerous. In 1340 Edward III defeated the French, and ten years later he routed the Spanish, capturing twenty-six of their forty ships. The Dutch, emerging as a major power, were trounced in both 1371 and 1387. In the 1387 engagement eighty Dutch ships out of a hundred were captured, yet later the Dutch navy became one of the most powerful in the world.

Further south, the Spanish and Portuguese were busy building the masted caravels with which they would discover America. Deep-sea trading was in its infancy, and as much commerce as possible was still conducted overland to avoid the liability of cargoes too often lost when ships foundered and sank at sea on or along the coasts they hugged in transit. That world, however, was about to change.

BELOW: Caravels in port, detail of an illustration by Theodore de Bry from 1594. The Spanish or Portuguese caravel (which the English called carvel), was a small, fast ship, one of the many types of vessel used by the Spanish Armada in 1588.

RIGHT: An aerial reconstruction of the battle of Lepanto, where, in 1571, an alliance of Spain, Venice, Genoa, and the Papal States decimated the Ottoman Turkish fleet.

CHAPTER TWO

BEYOND THE HORIZON
THE AGE OF EXPLORATION

Ship design in the West, where invention and innovation had been painfully slow, gradually improved. Meanwhile the Arabs, in advance of the European nations, had invented scientific instruments such as the astrolabe centuries before the great flood of applied science in eighteenth-century Europe. The Arabs were not fearful, as was the West, of falling off the edge of the earth—imagined to be flat until Copernicus and Galileo proved otherwise—and used their new technology to guide their ships reliably by the sun and the stars. In the South Pacific, the native peoples invented the outrigger canoe, which was, in pure shipbuilding terms, as efficient as the great vessels of Europe.

The arrogance and self-confidence of the European maritime nations often meant that if anything was likely to go wrong it did. Sea travel of all kinds, whether for the purpose of exploration, commerce, or war, was frequently a means of courting disaster. Until the formation of Lloyd's of London and their catalog of shipping for insurance purposes (undertaken in about 1764), few people knew how many ships had gone to the bottom of the sea.

Christopher Columbus

Although the Vikings were the first Europeans to discover America—having sailed there from Greenland—they did not remain long. Christopher Columbus came to America from Spain in 1492, thinking he had reached the East Indies. This historic journey was undertaken in three ships: his flagship *Santa María*, the *Pinta,* and the *Niña*. Unfortunately, the *Santa María* ran aground on Haiti and had to be abandoned. The crew of forty-four was left on the island to establish a fort—built from the wood of the *Santa María* herself—while Columbus returned in glory to Spain aboard the *Niña*.

Columbus seized numerous territories for Spain, first an island in the Bahamas which he called San Salvador, then Cuba, Haiti, and the Caribbean Islands. South America was discovered by Europeans in 1498; Florida was discovered in 1513 by the explorer Juan Ponce de Léon (who was searching for the mythical Fountain of Youth), by which time Columbus had died with his reputation in disgrace. Of particular value

BELOW: Contrary to the depiction of monsters on this sea map from 1572, knowledge usually meant safety at sea. As charts and navigation became more accurate, long voyages were proportionally less dangerous, unless in unknown waters.

LEFT: On August 3, 1492, Christopher Columbus set sail from Spain with his small fleet on an epic voyage of discovery.

were the discoveries of Mexico (1519) and Peru (1532–35), because it was there that the Spaniards found gold.

Spanish Bullion Ships

The Spanish explorers triumphed wherever they went because they had firearms, wore armor, and were ultimately more ruthless than the native Americans. They brought back gold in quantity and en route their treasure ships were frequently attacked by English privateers, often when they were close to land, where they were then grounded or sunk in shallow water. These were the first wrecks to be systematically plundered, and the economy (if such it could be called) of early Bermuda came to depend on Spanish ship casualties. The Spanish bullion ships are still a main target of bounty hunters, and as technology continues to advance more will be discovered and pillaged, even the vessels that lie at great depths.

In 1714, a convoy of twelve ships carrying gold bullion left Havana, Cuba, for Spain, but in the Bahama Channel they were struck by a hurricane. More than a thousand men

BELOW: The *Tolosa* and the *Guadalupe,* Spanish treasure ships, both sank in a hurricane in 1724 off the Dominican Republic. Both ships were loaded with gold bullion, coins, and four hundred tons of mercury worth millions of dollars. The two wrecks were discovered in 1977 in just forty feet of water.

RIGHT: Unlike other metals which corrode in salt water, gold can never be destroyed. Many of the gold coins recovered from Spanish bullion ships are in remarkably good condition.

perished at sea, although fifteen hundred managed to reach land. Salvage began immediately, and within a year officials reported that all the treasure had been recovered. Whether this was the truth or expedience, however, is impossible to say.

These ships were small by today's standards. The forecastle overhung the bow by nearly twelve feet, and the ship had a half-deck and a quarter-deck. The half-deck was a deck extending from the main mast aftward, situated between the smaller quarter-deck and the upper or main deck. The half-deck and the quarter-deck were later reduced to one deck, called the quarter-deck.

Columbus's ships were no longer than 128 feet, with a beam (width) of twenty-six feet. There were three masts and a bowsprit—a spar running from the stem of the vessel to which the foremost sail was attached. These ships were all made of wood and very vulnerable. Vessels of this type not only went to Newfoundland (for instance, the one captained by John Cabot in 1497) but rounded the Cape of Good Hope seeking a route to the lucrative trade among the East Indies' Spice Islands.

A New Breed of Warship

Ships gradually became larger—the pioneers in ship design were the French, the Genoese and the Venetians, who built merchant ships of up to 1,600 tons. A Portuguese carrack captured by the British carried six hundred to seven hundred passengers. The best known of the new race of warships was the *"Great Harry"* built by Henry VIII, launched in 1514 and destroyed by fire in 1553. These formidable warships had several tiers of guns, often with four masts, enormous forecastles, and deck-houses aft.

BELOW: Although English privateers often attacked Spanish vessels carrying gold bullion and other immensely valuable shipments such as quicksilver (mercury, used to amalgamate gold and silver from New World ore) the hostilities were not entirely one-sided. In this dramatic illustration, an English supply ship is captured by Spanish vessels.

There were four great European naval powers: the English, the French, the Dutch, and the Spaniards. Given the political and religious conflicts of the period, it was only a matter of time before one of the last three decided to make a determined effort to invade Britain. In 1588, the Spanish Armada was launched against England. The fleet was composed of 132 vessels ranging in size from the large galleons of about one thousand tons to smaller vessels of under one hundred tons. There were 8,050 sailors, 2,088 galley-slaves, 18,973 soldiers, and a mixed bag of 1,382 volunteers, including gentlemen, camp-followers, and sightseers. There were also 150 monks and the vicar-general of the Spanish Inquisition. England was defended by a force of only eighty vessels.

ABOVE: The embarkation of King Henry VIII at Dover in 1520. Ships designed at this time were larger and more elaborate; warships had several tiers of guns, often with four masts, and merchant ships were capable of carrying a vast quantity of cargo and numerous crew.

LEFT: One of the first of a new type of warship, the *"Great Harry"* was built on the orders of King Henry VIII, launched in 1514, and destroyed by fire in 1553.

CHART OF THE ARMADA'S COURSE.
Pine's Engraving, 1739, of Tapestry then in House of Lords.

ABOVE: A chart of the Armada's fateful course. Only half of the original fleet managed to return home; many ships not lost in battle were wrecked off the coast of Ireland, where the survivors were robbed and killed by local inhabitants.

LEFT: Had Britain been ruled by a weak monarch at the time of the invasion of the Spanish Armada, the outcome of world history might have been different. Queen Elizabeth I was not a ruler to be cowed, as is evident from this painting, known as the Armada Portrait.

ABOVE: In 1588, King Philip II of Spain launched the Spanish Armada to overthrow Queen Elizabeth I and establish himself on the throne of England.

After the Armada left home waters it was caught up in a storm and forced to seek shelter. However, the fleet soon reformed, entered the English Channel, and met the English, led by Lord Howard and his vice-admiral, Sir Francis Drake. The heavy, overcrowded Spanish ships were best suited to grappling and boarding opponents in hand-to-hand combat. However, the lighter English vessels avoided close-quarter fighting and used their superior speed to sail by the enemy and deliver devastating broadsides of cannon fire. Drake also resorted to the tactic of setting fire to some of his smaller ships and sailing them into the midst of the Spanish fleet. Frustrated, the Armada retired into the North Sea, and was once again dispersed by storms. The Spanish lost a great number of ships, many of which were wrecked as they tried to return home around the north of Scotland. Others were dashed onto the coast of Ireland, to the joy of the Irish who robbed and killed the survivors.

Spain's naval prestige was diminished, just as England's was enhanced, but she had more than enough wealth to build new ships. Spain remained a major power for another century, and her close relationship with the Netherlands meant that she remained a force to be reckoned with.

LEFT: The *Ark Royal*, the English flagship which led the battle against the Spanish Armada. On August 7, 1588, the English sent fireships into the Spanish fleet's anchorage, scattering them widely.

LEFT: Ocean-going vessels were vulnerable to small coastal pirate ships, such as these Chinese junks. Only with the arrival of the swift-traveling clipper ships could such pirates be outstripped.

International Trade

Ultimately trade was more important than war, and the most important international trade route was around the Cape of Good Hope to India and the East. The *Cabo Tormentoso* (cape of storms), also called the *Lion of the Sea* or the *Head of Africa,* was discovered by Bartholomew Diaz in 1488. Rounding the Cape in full and the discovery of a true passage to India was accomplished by Vasco da Gama on his epochal voyage from 1497 to 1499. Many ships later foundered on this profitable but dangerous route, and these inaccessible wrecks are likely to remain undisturbed forever, as are those of the ships that later braved the terrors of the Horn at the tip of South America. No one can ever truly know the number of ship casualties in these areas.

BELOW: Merchant ships were often attacked by pirates. The British East India Company had six hundred armed ships, although the addition of soldiers and extra supplies often made them slow and unwieldy.

LEFT: Pirates board a ship. In acts of piracy no rules of conduct applied, unlike naval warfare where prisoners were usually treated with the greatest courtesy.

FOLLOWING PAGE:
Traditional naval warfare was conducted with ships line abreast for broadside firing, but many engagements were conducted at close range where firepower was less important.

War at Sea

British-built, ocean-going ships soon became the best in the world. The British East India Company (1600–1874) had a fleet of six hundred armed ships, and successfully fought off Portuguese and Dutch interlopers who wanted a share of the colonial wealth. Not surprisingly there was constant tension between the great powers; wars broke out, some of them petty, some of them serious, and many were resolved by pitched sea battles.

The French were the chief rivals of the British in shipcraft, building bigger and faster warships to which Britain reacted with increasing alarm. Eighteenth-century fighting ships were categorized by the number of guns they carried, and the typical fighting ship at the beginning of the century had ninety guns. It was about 164 feet in length with a forty-seven-foot beam, and weighed about 1,570 tons. A new and powerful type of warship emerged called the frigate. Six to seven hundred tons and measuring 120 feet in length,the swift-moving, square-rigged frigate carried a bank of twenty-two to forty-four guns on a single flush gun deck.

The *Royal George*, launched in 1756, was longer, wider, carried a hundred guns, weighed over two thousand tons, and had a crew of 750. But this vessel was a failure, and became an early example of marine salvage. The *Royal George* heeled over at Spithead while undergoing minor repairs. Water entered and it went down immediately, drowning at least six hundred people. It had the tallest masts and squarest canvas of any ship in the navy to that point; 3,840 trees had been used to build it, each weighing more than a ton. The wreck was surveyed in 1817 using a diving bell, and parts of the vessel and some of the cargo were brought up between 1839 and 1842. For some reason best known to the authorities, the ship was then blown up using gunpowder ignited by electricity.

The French were now Britain's primary enemy, especially after the French Revolution when it was feared that the political "infection" would spread to England. Because they had a smaller navy, the French were inclined to avoid combat, but British tactics were superior and aimed at picking off the stragglers.

RIGHT: The French were the chief rivals of Britain on the sea, and the battle depicted here between the Dutch and French navies was a sign to Britain that enemies (and alliances) were not permanent.

LEFT: Many Dutch naval conflicts were sketched by the van de Veldes, a father-and-son team who worked on their drawings from small boats in the middle of the action. This scene depicts the battle of the Sont, which occurred in the Anglo-Dutch naval wars of the last half of the seventeenth century.

RIGHT: Joseph Turner's rendition of the battle of Trafalgar, viewed from Nelson's *Victory*. On October 21, 1805, the British fleet under Lord Nelson won a smashing victory over allied French and Spanish fleets.

RIGHT: In the battle of the First of June (June 3, 1794), the French ship *Le Vengeur* sinks after the French fleet was routed by an English force commanded by Admiral Richard Howe.

RIGHT: A portrait of Horatio Nelson by Lemuel Francis Abbott. Nelson's radical strategy at the battle of Trafalgar was to divide his fleet in half and penetrate the enemy in two places, a maneuver that resulted in the capture of twenty enemy ships.

The tradition of line astern fighting—making the broadside most effective—was sometimes broken by astute commanders.

In 1794, at the start of the open hostilities between England and France, 130 merchant ships sailed from the United States with a cargo of food for famine-stricken France. The French Navy put out to sea to guarantee the convoy's safe arrival, but British admiral Richard Howe intercepted the French warships in a four-day battle. The conflict ended when Howe, ignoring all convention, steered his fleet into the middle of the French ships so that every vessel was on its own, in what was known as a melee.

British seamanship and enterprise, *not* the quality of the ships (including the flagship, HMS *Victory*), secured Admiral Horatio Nelson's triumph at Trafalgar in 1805. An important factor in naval warfare at this time was that guns could not be trained to converge on a target less than 750 yards away. The range of effective fire was one thousand yards or a little over, and a vessel that maneuvered close to an enemy ship would rarely be dismasted or sunk.

The American Revolution

On the outbreak of the American Revolution in 1775, the American Navy consisted of two ships of twenty-four guns each, six brigs of ten to twelve guns, four sloops, and one other small vessel. All were lost in battle, and between 1780 and 1785 the United States did not have a navy. Yet John Paul Jones, given command of the sloop *Providence* in 1776, destroyed British fisheries in Nova Scotia, Canada, and captured sixteen British ships. In 1777, commanding the sloop *Ranger*, Jones cruised along the coast of Great Britain and sunk many vessels. Promoted to commodore and placed in command of a five-ship American-French force, he defeated the British man-of-war *Serapis* in its home waters. Jones later went to Russia to help the Russian Navy organize against the Turks.

The defeat of the *Serapis* was of serious concern to the British Navy, but deeper defects in its warships were highlighted in the War of 1812, when some of them were captured by the rapidly strengthening United States Navy. Several American vessels were manned by ex-Royal Navy men, and, when one British ship was captured, the prisoners, usually treated with courtesy, were put in irons to stop them fraternizing with their old comrades-in-arms.

ABOVE: John Paul Jones, the great American hero, leads his crew in the capture of the British vessel *Serapis* on September 23, 1779, during the Revolutionary War.

LEFT: From ancient times onward, diving for treasure was a hazardous business. The diving bell, invented in 1531, reduced some of the danger, as did the later brass-helmeted diving suit, but it was only with the invention of the aqualung in the 1930s that divers were able to obtain a high degree of freedom of movement.

LEFT: The subject of shipwrecks produced many great and moving paintings, among them *La Mort de Virginie* ("The Death of Virginia") by Claude Joseph Vernet (1714-89).

LEFT: Nathaniel Currier's lithograph illustrates Admiral Oliver Perry's important victory over British forces at Lake Erie in 1813, a turning point in the War of 1812 that compelled the British to abandon Detroit.

RIGHT: Stephen Decatur fighting the Algerians at Tripoli in 1804. The Tripolitan War, 1800–1815, was fought between the United States and the Barbary States of North Africa, following the refusal of the United States to pay additional money for protection against attacks of Barbary pirates on shipping.

LEFT: The destruction of the USS *Philadelphia* in Tripoli harbor in 1804, in a painting by Edward Moran. This incident occurred during America's first overseas land operation, when naval agent William Eaton, eight marines, a navy midshipman, and about a hundred mercenaries marched across six hundred miles of Libyan desert to restore the rightful ruler of Tripoli to his throne.

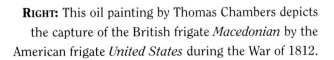

Perhaps the most dramatic encounter between American and British naval forces occurred at Lake Erie on September 10, 1813. The British had occupied Detroit in August, 1812, and had built a fleet for action on the Great Lakes. In March of 1813, Commodore Oliver Hazard Perry and a force of men arrived at Erie, Pennsylvania, to build a fleet to fight the British. Perry's force consisted of nine vessels mounting fifty-four guns and was opposed by six vessels mounting sixty-three guns. The British concentrated their fire on Perry's flagship, the *Lawrence*, which was badly mauled. Perry transferred his flag to the *Niagara*, and, after a sustained engagement, the British flagship, HMS *Detroit*, surrendered with three other vessels. The remaining two tried to escape but were captured. Within three weeks the British had evacuated Detroit.

However, notwithstanding this setback, the Battle of Trafalgar highlighted the fact that Britain was the only major naval power in the world. For more than a hundred years there were no great sea battles, and the Royal Navy, unchallenged, secured the oceans for conquest and colonization. Other European nations did their best. Germany established footholds in Africa; France had control over the most inhospitable parts of northern and central Africa; Belgium took the Congo; Portugal and Spain also had large territories; and the adventurous Dutch made their mark in the East Indies, among the most profitable of all colonies.

RIGHT: This oil painting by Thomas Chambers depicts the capture of the British frigate *Macedonian* by the American frigate *United States* during the War of 1812.

Recoveries and Restorations

Over the centuries, countless merchant and naval vessels sunk to the bottom of the sea. Many have been recovered, such as Henry VIII's *Mary Rose*, a four-masted, sixty-ton vessel built in 1529, which sank in 1545 when she suddenly heeled over in shallow waters off Portsmouth, possibly because water had entered the gun-ports. Her hull was discovered in 1968, almost intact under fifteen feet of mud, and she has since been painstakingly restored. The Swedish warship the *Wasa*, built as a prestige symbol by a powerful nation, went down in 1628 and was raised in amazing condition (preserved by the benign waters of the Baltic) in 1959. In its restored state the *Wasa* is a monument to what a dedicated marine archaeological team can do.

Sometimes when a wreck is discovered it is simply not financially viable to salvage. However, one wreck well worth recovering was HMS *Lutine*, a French ship captured by the British, which was carrying a great quantity of bullion and coin—the property of various merchants. It went down off Holland in 1799 carrying a cargo insured by Lloyd's of London. Although the Dutch claimed the wreck, a third of the salvage was granted in 1801 to a group of bullion divers. After more than half a century, in 1857 the Dutch government agreed to allow Lloyd's half of what remained of the cargo. By 1859, Lloyd's had received £22,162 of an estimated one hundred thousand pounds recovered from the seabed. More than a million pounds remains underwater.

In 1748 the Dutch ship *Amsterdam*, a-six-to-seven-hundred-ton vessel bound for Batavia in the Dutch East Indies, went aground on the Sussex coast of the English Channel. Besides the conventional cargo of gold bullion there were "a great many thousand dozen" bottles of wine. The Mayor of Hastings tried to acquire some, reckoning it would cost him a shilling a bottle. In due course the sea covered the ship, and it was not seen again for more than seventy years.

In 1810, a search was made again for the *Amsterdam,* without success, but a low tide in 1827 revealed the wreck and enabled the locals to indulge in looting—only to find that the Lord Warden of the Cinque ports (an ancient honorary title once held by Sir Winston Churchill) claimed the booty. There matters rested until 1969 when, during a phenomenally low tide, a local contractor busy on a new sewage outtake sent in bulldozers, uncovering cannons and wine. Many of the bottles were intact, and despite the raw sewage in the vicinity local boys began searching the uncovered wreck, drinking the wine (which was not unlike claret), and distributing odds and ends to those who would part with small silver coins. It took a long time to restore order and, although the Dutch Government made a valid claim for the ship and its contents, much had been taken or destroyed. Soon the sea covered the wreck once again.

BELOW: Wrecks contain pockets of history in many shapes and forms. These glasses are from the *Tolosa,* one of two Spanish bullion ships sunk in 1724.

ABOVE: These typical seventeenth-century galleons illustrate the fact that innovations in ship design were slow to develop, and would remain so until the age of iron and steam.

Innovations in Technology

The technology of marine navigation paralleled innovations in ship design and increased traffic, both military and commercial, on the world's oceans. Around 1400 the first magnetic compass (previously known to the Chinese in A.D. 121) was used in the West. Although a ship could be navigated by the sun and the stars, Columbus had use of only a compass and possibly a cross staff (utilized to measure altitudes at sea, therefore establishing the position of the ship in relation to known star clusters, particularly the sun and the constellation known as Little Bear, or Ursa Minor), in addition to a largely dubious chart. He could check the latitude of his vessels (north or south) but not their longitude (east or west).

The back staff, which was used while positioned with one's back to the sun, was invented in 1590, replacing the cross staff, which had been used facing the sun—a method that had proved both inconvenient and dangerous to the observer's eyes. In 1731, the British scientist John Hadley invented the reflecting octant. By using a system of mirrors, the observer then did not have to try and face two ways at once. (The octant, sextant, and quadrant belong to the same family—the octant is an eighth of a circle, the sextant a sixth, the quadrant a quarter.) Columbus and his contemporaries may have used a log—a piece of wood on a line thrown overboard and drifted past two observers posted a known distance apart—to calculate the speed of his ships.

In 1714, a British organization called the Commissioners for the Discovery of Longitude at Sea offered £2,000—then an immense sum of money—to anyone who could find a solution to the query posed in their title. Logarithms as a navigational aid had been discovered in 1614; no one knew what a nautical mile was until 1637. Finding the correct longitude, naturally, depended on knowing the exact time. Thus it was a clock maker, John Harrison, who in 1735 invented the marine chronometer, the ultimate in clockwork technology, and this worked so well that it was used almost unchanged for the next two hundred years.

A sea captain could now find out exactly where he was located, and charts were published which began to have real value. The sea was now no longer quite so mysterious, though it was still dangerous. With the great increase in colonization, trade, and exploration in the nineteenth century, disasters at sea not only continued—they multiplied.

BELOW: Dismasting was the greatest danger faced by a sailing ship. Underwater obstacles could often be ridden over by a wooden ship without sinking the vessel, but when her masts had gone, either in storms or in fighting, a ship was truly at the mercy of the waves.

CHAPTER THREE

IRON AND STEAM

INDUSTRIAL REVOLUTION AT SEA

As a new nation without strong traditional roots, the United States was able to address many diverse issues with objectivity and dispatch. Seeking a fast merchant vessel, ship designers developed the first of the Yankee clippers in 1833. The new ship had large sails, a long, slender hull, and a small crew, which saved weight on provisions. Clipper ships made no pretense to be armed merchants like the East Indiamen, so they were not loaded down with cannon and soldiers.

The clipper ship was speedily adopted by the British, but shipyards were unable to come up with anything remotely equal to the American vessels, and naval engineers were further handicapped by the archaic Navigation Acts. Only in 1849, when these laws were repealed, could clippers from the River Clyde and Aberdeen finally compete in international waters. British clippers brought the early teas from China and wool from Australia, and speed was of the essence on these routes. These clippers were small, averaging seven hundred tons, and the trip from China took about three months. The tea was packed in Chinese porcelain containers, which doubled as ballast and which are now extremely valuable.

The British East India Company enjoyed a monopoly of trade with the Far East until 1833, when its charter was revised. Their ships were "snugged down" for the night, that is, sail and speed were reduced, and progress was stately. In 1842 Queen Victoria visited Scotland in her yacht, which was towed by a naval steamer. She returned in a fast sailing ship, the *Trident*, which left both the naval steamer and yacht well behind. Speedy passage was required—or demanded, as in the case of the Queen—by passengers and especially by the mail services, where the American-built packets were supreme.

BELOW: One of the first iron-hull ships, *The Great Eastern,* was launched in 1857 and remained in service until 1889.

The age of the British tea-clipper was short—1849 to 1875. The cutting of the Suez Canal in 1869, a passage navigable only by steamships, marked the beginning of the end for the tea-clipper. The *Cutty Sark,* a restored tea-clipper now moored near London, was actually built the year that the Suez Canal opened.

LEFT: Despite the coming of steam, sailing ships were still being built and launched and were even preferred for certain duties. In this 1860 lithograph, a sailing ship is caught in an Arctic storm.

RIGHT: The clipper *Comet* of New York in a storm. Lithograph by Nathaniel Currier, 1855.

ABOVE: One of the greatest of all shipwreck paintings, Théodore Géricault's *The Raft of the "Medusa"* depicts a catastrophe in which survivors of the ship *Medusa* drifted across the sea for twenty-seven days. The violence of the painting shocked viewers when it was exhibited at the Louvre in 1819.

RIGHT: The wreck of the steamship *San Francisco* in 1853, lithograph by Nathaniel Currier, 1854.

From Sail to Steam

The change from sail to steam and from wood to iron and steel took place gradually. There was a strong opposition lobby, and the "Wooden Walls of Old England"—the British navy that had kept foreigners out—took a long time to fall.

The first practical steam vessel was the *Charlotte Dundas* of 1801, used successfully as a tug. Robert Fulton, also the inventor of the torpedo, launched a steam vessel on the Hudson River in 1807, and by 1812 a steamboat called the *Comet* plied the River Clyde in Scotland. The first steamship recorded by Lloyd's was the 294-ton *James Watt*, launched in 1822. The first steamship to cross the Atlantic was the *Sirius*, built in 1837. However, as late as 1859 the 121-gun *Victoria*, an old-fashioned wooden three-decker warship with sails only, was launched.

For many years the naval authorities did not see a future for the steam engine except for powering tugboats. It was considered to be vulnerable, and this was certainly true for the first steamships, the paddle-steamers, whose paddle wheels interfered with steering and whose engines necessitated large supplies of bulky fuel. In war, a well-aimed cannon could destroy a paddle with one shot, immediately rendering the ship unseaworthy.

BELOW: Fire raged aboard the steamship *Lexington* in Long Island Sound, January 13, 1840. The dramatic lithograph is by Nathaniel Currier.

RIGHT: Rounding Cape Horn was a very dangerous undertaking for any sailing vessel. This illustration by Currier & Ives shows the clipper *Red Jacket* in ice off Cape Horn in 1854, during her voyage from Australia to Liverpool with a cargo of wool.

ABOVE: The burning of the Yankee clipper *Golden Light* in February, 1853. Because of their lightweight structure, clipper ships were more vulnerable to fire than heavier vessels. Lithograph by Nathaniel Currier.

RIGHT: A steamship could often power its way out of an Arctic ice field, whereas a sailing ship would be marooned. Ice-breaking vessels were only introduced in 1875.

LEFT: Despite the added strength of steel construction and the power of steam propulsion, an early twentieth-century ship was still no match for the force of a storm at sea.

The Iron Ships

Many pointed to the fully rigged ironclad as the *real* future of warships. In 1859, the French took a traditional two-decker, cut off the top deck, and armor-plated the rest. The Royal Navy retaliated with the epoch-making *Warrior,* about which a modern naval historian said that when she was put into commission she could have taken on the navies of the world single-handed and beaten them all. The *Warrior* was built on an iron frame, divided into watertight compartments by bulkheads. She was 9,140 tons, 380-feet long, with a beam of fifty-eight feet, had four-and-a-half inch armor which could resist the heaviest gun afloat (the hundred-pounder, of which she herself carried eleven), and a crew of 705. She had a powerful engine that could make more than fourteen knots. The *Warrior* was ordered in 1859, launched in 1861, and obsolete by 1884.

The ultimate iron ship was the *Great Eastern.* Put in hand in 1854 and launched in 1857, her iron hull weighed 6,250 tons and was constructed from thirty thousand small plates seamed together with three million rivets. Its total tonnage was 23,000, and the vessel was 680-feet long, with both screw and paddle engines. It used immense quantities of coal— approximately 280 tons a day—and made a speed of fourteen knots. Despite its structural innovations, the *Great Eastern* was not a success, and after participating in the laying of cables for the transatlantic telegraph, it was pressed into use as a dancing saloon. When the boat was finally broken up for scrap in 1889, it was found that the hull was still in excellent condition, and the ship may well have been truly unsinkable.

BELOW: The historic battle between the ironclads *Merrimack* and *Monitor,* March 9, 1862, at the beginning of the Civil War. The two ships bombarded each other for four hours, but the battle was a draw.

A Time of Change

Changes in ship building were coming fast. During the Civil War, inventor John Ericsson persuaded the Federal authorities to build a new style of fighting ship, the ironclad monitor. Launched in 1862, the original *Monitor* had complete armor above the waterline, a low silhouette, and a revolving gun-turret—the most significant advance in sea warfare since the invention of gunpowder. This innovation made the fitting of mast and sail impossible, so the new ship was driven by steam power, with a screw propeller.

The British immediately saw the possibilities of the monitor, and in 1869 they launched the *Captain*. This ship had four twenty-five-ton guns in two turrets, and weighed 4,272 tons, but it was fully rigged. The *Captain* proved to be a disaster; speedily and badly designed, she capsized in a squall off Cape Finisterre in 1870. As soon as the edge of the deck dipped under water the boat toppled over and most of the five hundred men aboard perished. The *Glatton* and the *Devastation*, both launched by Britain in 1871, were true turret-ships, each with only one mast for signaling purposes.

Threats from Continental navies, whether actual or perceived, were taken seriously. As early as 1838 it was feared that Britain would lose her supremacy. The French and Russians were building up sea power at great speed, and an alliance between the two

ABOVE: This hand-colored photograph, taken in 1862, shows the USS *Cairo* at patrol on the Mississippi River. The *Cairo* was one of a flotilla of twelve ironclad gunboats in the fleet of Commodore A. H. Foote during the Civil War.

FOLLOWING PAGE: The Great Fight at Charleston, South Carolina, April 7, 1863. Here, Union and Confederate ironclads and monitors clash on the river near Fort Sumter.

countries meant that their combined navies would be stronger than the British forces. The year 1871 saw the unification of Italy and the formation of the German Empire, both of which would come to have strong fleets.

There was also a threat to Britain from across the Atlantic. Using mass-production methods unique to the United States, and a new system of interchangeable parts—standardized components that simplified replacement and manufacture—the United States had quickly built up a formidable fighting force. It is sometimes forgotten that in the late nineteenth century there was a good chance of a war between Britain and America resulting from a bitter frontier dispute in Venezuela, and that the United States prepared for a British attack coming through Canada.

In any event, British fears at that time were needless. Her huge warships were never used in combat. This was indeed fortunate for them, because many were old and obsolete, and the Royal Navy had continued to conform to a structure which was largely leftover from the Napoleonic Wars.

The *Maine* Incident

Unlike the Royal Navy at that time, the American naval forces saw military action. In 1898, the 6,682-ton battleship *Maine* was stationed in Havana to protect the lives of Americans in Cuba after recent riots. The *Maine* was the first true American battleship,

ABOVE: In 1898, the 6,682-ton battleship USS *Maine*, stationed in Havana to protect the lives of Americans in Cuba after recent riots, was blown up in the harbor of Havana, with great loss of life. The Spanish-American War followed sixty-nine days later.

LEFT: The last resort for a ship caught in a storm was to cut away the masts. This made the ship less vulnerable, though it also meant that if the weather cleared there would be no way to guide or power the vessel.

RIGHT: The *Underley,* built in 1866 and wrecked off the Isle of Wight, England, was an accident with minor loss of life. Only one person, a steward, died, but there certainly would have been more casualties if the gunpowder in the cargo hold had exploded.

BELOW: The unexpected could often cause disaster at sea. Derelict ships and even whales, could be a deadly threat, even to steamships.

well-armed with machine guns and torpedoes, and capable of a speed of eighteen knots. War between the occupying colonial power, Spain, and the United States was being fostered by the newspaper tycoon William Randolph Hearst, who opened the issue in a headline declaring "500 Women Butchered." There was no evidence of wrongdoing, but when one of Hearst's reporters telegraphed his editor, saying that there was no real story in Cuba, Hearst responded: "You furnish the story. I'll furnish the war."

There was no friction between the *Maine* and the Cuban authorities; relations were cordial, even friendly, but insults were hurled at the crew of the *Maine* by passengers on a ferry, and steam was kept up and shells for the guns were readied. The captain was suddenly startled by "a bursting, rending, and crashing sound or roar of immense volume," which shattered windows in Havana and destroyed the *Maine*'s power plant. Soon a fire was raging out of control. Twelve of the fifteen lifeboats were too badly damaged to be lowered; 261 men died, ninety-four were saved. At first it was believed that an accident had occurred, but there was government pressure in Washington to prove otherwise. The Assistant Secretary of the Navy, Theodore Roosevelt, believed that the nation wanted a war and "Spain will do fine." A court of inquiry later decided that the ship had been struck by a mine, because the explosion had forced the steel plates inwards. War followed sixty-nine days after the *Maine* was sunk.

It has come to be believed that the Spanish government was not involved, and that the mine—if there was one—was placed by a dissident. Some of the crew reported hearing two explosions, but an exploding mine usually results in a large number of dead fish, and none were found when the ship went down. The *Maine* was raised in 1911 and the findings of the original inquiry were confirmed. It was then sunk in deep water, thus preventing further examination.

Innovations in Engineering

In Britain, there is no doubt that smaller vessels were more useful in tackling the "bush wars" that supervision by the British Empire entailed. The first time a steamship was used in war was in 1824 when a small vessel, the *Diana*, was flung into the Burmese War of 1824–26. The "fire-ship" of the "wild foreigners" was regarded with awe, though most of the action was done by three gun-boats which took on and defeated several hundred Burmese war boats. During the Crimean War, "floating batteries," heavy guns mounted and towed on sea-going platforms, were used by the French and British allies against the Russians, but these proved unstable and, at length, unnecessary.

There was great reluctance to use metal instead of wood in both military and merchant ships. The iron hull was initially developed to withstand the vibration of the steam engine, and was replaced by steel between 1875 and 1880. The iron hull was also suitable for sailing ships, though there were

LEFT: In a ship similar to this one, composer Richard Wagner thought himself near death during a violent storm in the North Sea, but he lived to use his experience as the inspiration for his well-known opera, *The Flying Dutchman* (1840).

objections that it would corrode too easily and would also fracture on relatively small underwater hazards which a wooden ship would ride over undamaged.

As long as steam engines were unreliable, and until paddles were discarded in favor of the screw propeller (first patented in 1836), steamships were fully rigged. Even when engines became efficient, some sails were kept to steady the ship. But as speeds increased, the sails proved a hindrance rather than an asset, and there was often only an ill-trained crew to manipulate them. Because of the importance of coaling—steamships could not carry sufficient fuel to power their engines without frequent stops to replenish the supply—many boats had to take indirect courses to their destinations.

The Aftermath of Innovation

This combination of "sail and steam" was very effective, but it could also be catastrophic. The introduction of new and untried vessels, the adaptation of unsuitable sailing ships for steam engines, the taking-on of crew who were not experienced sailors or seamen brought about maritime disasters on the largest scale to date. There were massive ship losses due to incompetence, greed, insurance fraud, and human error. Ships were still active on the seas which were not merely old but ancient.

ABOVE: The dramatic rescue of eleven persons from the wreck of the American vessel *Alarm*, near Belfast.

RIGHT: When disaster strikes at sea, help is sometimes forthcoming from other vessels. But it is often the rescuers who are in the most peril, as is evident from this engraving, where men attempting to help the crew of the *Elizabeth* are themselves at risk.

Lloyd's Register of Shipping, 1909–10, listed the *Olivia*, 1819, as still in operation, and the schooner *Polly*, built in 1805, was still sailing in 1902.

Between 1854 and 1879 a total of 49,322 British vessels were lost at sea. These are official figures published in 1883, and recent research by Lloyd's reported that there were 120,000 wrecks around the shores of Great Britain. These include accidents deliberately contrived by wreckers on the shore, who moved warning beacons—waiting like vultures when there was a storm and the likelihood of a shipwreck. The center of this industry was Cornwall, in the extreme southwest of the country, a poor county dependent on agriculture, tin mining, and fishing.

Through an uncensored press, especially in the United States and Britain, the horrible details of increasingly frequent shipwrecks were revealed to the public eye. Myths were debunked almost weekly. The "women and children first" rule was one of the first casualties; the ablest and the strongest boarded the lifeboats—if indeed there were lifeboats still in operation, for in collisions they were the first things to be crushed, and their lowering devices were often only operable when the ship was level and not dipping into the water at an incredible angle.

BELOW: During the Opium Wars between Britain and China (1839–42) many British transport ships were sunk in typhoons, especially in the China Sea, with great loss of life.

LEFT: The paddle steamers of the early nineteenth century were notoriously difficult to steer. Here, the naval training ship HMS *Racer* has run aground on Ryde Sands.

LEFT: The steamship *Rangoon* was fortunate that passengers and crew were able to escape before it went under. The captain ignored beacons, hit rocks, and although he ordered the firing of rockets and a signal gun to summon help, no one responded.

The *Arctic* and the *Vesta*

In 1850, the American vessel *Arctic* was launched. It was one of the earliest luxury liners, with heat from its boilers warming various sections of the ship. The *Arctic* established a world record for speed in 1852, when it made the New York to Liverpool run in only ten days. Built without watertight bulkheads, it had only two steam pumps and four hand pumps for emergencies. If water came in the hull in quantity, it would be totally flooded. A disaster was waiting to happen.

ABOVE: The USS *Republic,* one of the great sailing vessels that marked the United States as an increasingly powerful maritime nation.

In 1854, the *Arctic* set off as usual from Liverpool to New York. Fog arrived, but the captain continued at full speed, thirteen knots. Steaming out of the fog at ten knots came a French ship, the *Vesta,* and the two ships collided. *Vesta* lost ten feet of her bow, but the *Arctic* seemed undamaged. The captain of the American ship realized that he ought to assist the *Vesta,* especially since one of her lifeboats had capsized, drowning several passengers. As the *Arctic*'s rescue boat was lowered, it was then realized that the *Arctic* itself was holed in three places—one hole was five feet wide—and water was rushing in. The captain decided to man the pumps and head for land, leaving the *Vesta* to its own fate. As he ordered full steam ahead the *Arctic* smashed into the second *Vesta* lifeboat.

Thirty-five miles from land, the *Arctic's* paddles stopped, and the order was given to abandon ship; there were not enough boats, so it was decided to make a raft. The stokers headed for the lifeboats, and when a crewman took a revolver to stop them so that women and children could get away he was hit on the head with

a shovel and killed. Other crew members lowered a boat, reassuring the passengers that they were merely inspecting the damage, and then rowed away. There were 250 passengers, but one remaining boat. All set to work on the raft, but it was too late and shortly afterward the ship went down. One of the survivors was the captain, who observed from the water, "a most awful and heartrending scene . . . two hundred men, women and children were struggling together amidst pieces of wreck of every kind calling on each other for help, and imploring God to assist them. Such an appalling scene: May God preserve me from ever witnessing it again."

Most of the men, women, and children who had set out from Liverpool drowned. Eight-five of the 435 aboard lived, and most of these survivors, including the captain, were rescued the following day. The *Vesta* limped into port relatively undamaged, since it was fitted out with watertight bulkheads and could have taken on the crew and passengers of the *Arctic*. The captain of the *Arctic* went into the marine insurance business after a mild reproof.

ABOVE: By the end of the nineteenth century, the United States had emerged as a naval power of significance. This unarmored cruiser, an American warship of the 1890s, is accompanied by several smaller vessels.

Man-Made Disasters

The 3,607-ton *Atlantic* set out from Britain in 1873 with an inadequate supply of coal and food. It was decided by her captain to divert to Halifax, Nova Scotia, refuel there, and continue on to New York. This meant that he would have to tackle an unknown sea with imponderable hazards. However, because the boat needed to stay on schedule, it was full speed ahead. A warning light was ignored as the captain believed he was somewhere else. In due course the ship hit rocks and sank. Three hundred people were drowned immediately, and the remaining crew commandeered the lifeboats—those which could still be launched, since the rest were already underwater. Some survivors were saved by clinging to a rock and were eventually rescued by fishing boats. Of the 931 who were aboard, 481 perished. No women—and only one child—survived. The captain had his license revoked for two years.

The *Cospatrick,* launched in 1856, sailed in 1874 from Britain to New Zealand with 429 emigrants. The forecastle contained rope, paint, varnish, kerosene, coal, and a large quantity of alcohol. It also contained the water pump, so that when the forecastle went up in flames there was nothing available with which to fight the fire. Through a misunderstanding the helmsman turned the ship into the wind, and it quickly became a fireball. Although two boats were launched, only three out of a crew of forty-four survived after horrendous experiences including cannibalism. Not one of the passengers on board was saved.

In 1871, the all-iron steamship *Megoera* was on a voyage from England to Australia carrying about four hundred people when she sprang a leak. It was discovered that her bottom was almost eaten away by corrosion and subsequent investigation revealed that the ship had been reported unfit for service four years earlier.

Many emigrants from Europe to the United States and Canada simply did not reach their destinations. In 1852 the steamship *St. George*, bound from Liverpool to New York with Irish emigrants, was destroyed by fire at sea. On a voyage from Liverpool to Quebec in 1863 with 445 passengers and crew the *Anglo Saxon* smashed up against rocks near shore. Most of the pas-

sengers had intended to settle in the Canadian West, but 227 were drowned en route in this wreck.

Some sea disasters—in the following case really only a mishap—received massive newspaper coverage. In 1886, the steam-yacht *Aloa* was built for William K. Vanderbilt, a son of American railroad magnate Cornelius Vanderbilt, at a cost of half a million dollars. On her way to Newport, Rhode Island, in 1892 the *Aloa* became fogbound, anchored, and was hit by a steamer plying between New York and Boston. There were no casualties and Vanderbilt and his guests were safely taken off their ship. Vanderbilt's first act upon landing was to telephone and order a new yacht. Four days after the collision, the wreck of the *Aloa* was struck by a vessel carrying coal. The *Aloa* was then judged to be a danger to shipping traffic and was blown up to avoid further damage.

The *Hunley*

In May of 1995, the submarine *Hunley* was discovered off the coast of South Carolina after a twenty-three-year search carried out by Clive Cussler, author of *Raise the Titanic*, and a team from the University of South Carolina. This unique ship was used by the Confederates in the Civil War and was the first submarine to sink another vessel. The submarine was adapted from a boiler twenty-five-feet long, and in its trials it

LEFT: When a shipwreck was considered to be hazardous to other ocean-going traffic, it was burned. In this Currier & Ives lithograph, American whaling ships crushed by ice are set on fire to avoid further tragedies at sea.

had been sunk three times with the loss of thirty lives. Its armament was a wooden spar tipped with a hundred pounds of gunpowder. During its final moments, the gunpowder spar was rammed into the stern of the Union frigate USS *Housatonic*. The *Hunley* backed away, and the gunpowder was triggered with the aid of a rope. The *Housatonic* was sunk, but it is highly likely that shock waves from the explosion finished off the *Hunley*.

Acts of God

No matter how able the captain, hurricanes and typhoons—where waves rise up to a height of one hundred feet—could destroy the best-built steamships in a matter of minutes. The *Rhone* was a mail-carrying passenger vessel of 2,738 tons, launched in 1865, and capable of the very swift speed of eighteen knots. She was designed for long transatlantic trips, coaling at St. Thomas in the US Virgin Islands. Anchored outside

BELOW: In this dramatic engraving, sailing ships are endangered by fantastic ice formations near Spitsbergen, a large island in the Arctic Ocean which served as the starting point for polar expeditions by Roald Amundsen and Richard Byrd, among others.

LEFT: As ships ventured further into the North Atlantic, icebergs became an increasing danger. This illustration shows the bow of the *Arizona* after her collision with an iceberg.

FOLLOWING PAGE: The Mississippi River in time of war. Naval warfare was carried out on the Mississippi as well as on the open seas.

Great Harbor, St. Thomas, she was hit by a sudden hurricane, and in trying to head for open water in order to ride out the storm her superheated boilers exploded, breaking the ship in half and forcing it up against razor-sharp rocks. Seventy-five ships had been lost previously in this "safe" anchorage over the years.

Early bounty hunters looted the *Rhone* of china, crystal, and much bullion, and the vessel received additional exposure in 1976 when it was used in the film *The Deep*. Unlike many wrecks, the *Rhone* is accessible. She lies in clear water not deeper than eighty-two feet, is safe for divers, and has become a popular tourist attraction.

Perils of the Inland Sea

Ships can sink anywhere. Stretches of inland water can be as dangerous as the mid-Atlantic, often more so, because most of them are not salt water, which offers a degree of buoyancy. Nowhere is this more true than the Great Lakes, where more than five hundred shipwrecks have been recorded. Fresh water is whipped up more quickly by the wind, and the distances between wave peaks is smaller. In the sea a ship can ride the waves—up with a peak, down into the trough—but in many inland seas there is simply not sufficient space between the waves to do this. Waves on the Great Lakes can rise to forty-three feet, a dangerous height for many vessels.

One of the largest ships to go down was the American steamer *Lady Elgin*, which sank in Lake Michigan after a collision with a schooner. Of the 385 people on board, 287 were lost. More typical was the *Sweepstakes*, a schooner built in Ontario in 1867 for the increasing cross-lake trade. It sank in 1896 in mysterious circumstances while carrying a cargo of coal. Nearby lies the *City of Grand Rapids*, built in 1879 and burned out and grounded in 1907, as well as the *Arabia*, downed in a gale in 1884 and discovered only by reason of its cargo: it was carrying 20,000 bushels of corn, and fish caught in the area at that time were found to have corn in their stomachs. Many

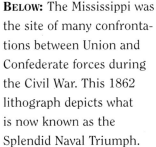

BELOW: The Mississippi was the site of many confrontations between Union and Confederate forces during the Civil War. This 1862 lithograph depicts what is now known as the Splendid Naval Triumph.

divers have died trying to explore the *Arabia*, which lies in deceptively deep, clear water.

Many great inland seas, such as the Caspian Sea and Lake Lagoda in Russia, have proved treacherous even to large ships, and in remote places there is often no record of what ships sailed and when and how many have sunk without survivors. Even stranger are those ships which have not sunk but that are without survivors (these are known as derelicts and their routes are often fully charted), such as the *Marie Celeste*, but the world of marine disasters is full of such oddities. There is, for example, the ship where the sailors would not do their duties because they claimed that there were two witches in the hold. To claim insurance, many unscrupulous shipping lines sent their vessels to certain doom by various strata-gems such as inadequate fuel, inexperienced crews, incompetent captains, and unsafe vessels which may have been tampered with prior to sailing.

Some ships have gone down without loss of life and near to land because it was financially convenient for them to do so. One of the strangest of these incidents occurred when a crew who hated and feared their captain decided to drill holes in the hull so that he was obliged to beach the vessel, whereupon they ran away. Mutiny would have been an easier option, except that the dissatisfied sailors would have been hanged.

As the nineteenth century drew to a close, there were great improvements in technology, and it was believed that the unsinkable ship would soon arrive. This ship would be bigger than anything that had come before—perhaps a floating palace, some said—and the power of the new steam turbine engine would make it go even faster. This assumption, however, was incorrect.

ABOVE: The Great Lakes are a graveyard for hundreds of ships, many of the wrecks are not too deep and are accessible to novice divers. Great Lake freighters capable of carrying 12,500 tons of coal were specialty vessels specifically designed for conditions on the inland seas.

CHAPTER FOUR

MODERN TIMES

INTRODUCING THE "UNSINKABLE SHIP"

The age of steel brought new confidence to ship design, materials, and performance. With bulkheads—hulls divided into watertight compartments—a double bottom, and a rust-proof, stable metal for construction, there was good reason to believe that ships could be built to survive anything.

Shipbuilding was now a massive industry with unrivaled tools and skills at its disposal. From the end of the 1880s onward, twin-screw propulsion provided much higher speeds, and the introduction of the steam turbine in the 1890s further enabled shipping lines to promote their lucrative

ABOVE: Although ships could be sunk by negligence, insurance fraud, or enemy action, the greatest threat was posed by the weather. In this illustration, the American steamer *Yantic* is caught in a cyclone.

RIGHT: The wrecks of the *Luther Little* and *Hesper* create a ghostly scene at Wiscasset, Maine.

ABOVE: A battle near Chemulpo, Korea, in 1904, during the Russo-Japanese War. The Japanese used torpedo boats to destroy Russian warships in their "safe" anchorages before war was actually declared, a tactic which was repeated by the Japanese during their attack on Pearl Harbor, December 7, 1941.

transatlantic route. Money was no object to many of their passengers, and the new breed of luxury ocean liners would certainly not be used by penniless emigrants.

However, despite hopes that a new era of safe sea travel had begun for the world, there were a great number of marine disasters in the 1890s, often close to land. In 1890, the 3,484-ton steamer *Quetta* bound for India and England from Queensland, Australia, struck a rock in a narrow channel and went down in three minutes, leaving 133 survivors out of 291. On the other side of Australia in 1894, a New Zealand-bound steamship called the *Wairarapa* smashed into cliffs in thick fog, and sixteen horses being transported on board only added to the ensuing confusion. Even close to land ninety-seven people died. Again in Australian waters, the *Catterthun* struck rocks in 1895; her Chinese crew panicked, and sixty-five lives were lost. Since the *Catterthun* went down with £11,000 in sovereigns, special gear was brought from England that allowed divers to recover £9,000 before the ship broke up.

The Wireless Telegraph

Radio transformed safety at sea. In 1897, Guglielmo Marconi started a company for sending wireless messages for short distances between ship and shore. One of his first customers was the East Goodwin lightship, which was equipped with radio at the end of 1898. This was providential, as it was rammed by a steamship three months later and so sent out the first radio distress call in history. Tugs were dispatched and the lightship, damaged but still afloat, was brought to safety.

Much more dramatic was the collision between the White Star liner *Republic* and the emigrant ship *Florida* twenty-six miles off Nantucket. The *Republic* sent out a distress call, a flotilla of ships arrived, and the rescue was accomplished easily. This encouraged all nervous sea travelers to take heart, but it also made the shipping authorities overconfident. If there should be a collision at sea the presence of a radio operator would soon bring help, especially since the sea lanes were increasingly crowded and there was sure to be another ship in the vicinity.

RIGHT: The defeat of the Russian fleet by the Japanese Navy in 1905. The Russian fleet was virtually annihilated by the Japanese, and Japan achieved almost instantaneous status as an international naval power.

RIGHT: The wreck of a ship that ran around in 1906, drowning six people, near Takaroa Atoll, in Tuamotus, Polynesia.

RIGHT: The British express liner *Titanic*, carrying 1,517 people, sank on April 14, 1912, in the North Atlantic on its maiden voyage, after colliding with an iceberg. Painting by H. J. Jansen, Antwerp, 1913.

ABOVE: The *Titanic* had sixteen lifeboats and four collapsibles. These could hold 1,178 of the 2,207 aboard, if all were still functional. In the end, only 705 people survived the voyage.

There were tragedies in distant places no one had ever heard of. Some were barely reported in the media or relegated to inside pages of the newspapers, including the epic naval encounters that occurred during the Russo-Japanese War from 1904 to 1905, wherein the Russian fleet was eventually destroyed. At the outset of the war the Japanese used torpedo boats as well as minefields to sink the Russian ships in their "safe" anchorage. In pitched sea battles the Japanese also proved superior, and the scale of the Russian losses was very high. So great was Russia's hysteria that reinforcements from the Balkan fleet on their way to the Far East bombarded British fishing boats in the North Sea in the belief that they were Japanese torpedo boats. Several British fishermen were killed, nearly precipitating a war with Russia.

The "Unsinkable" *Titanic*

In any event, a disaster in April of 1912 eclipsed every previous sea tragedy—this was the sinking of the *Titanic*, the ship "God Himself could not sink." More books have been written about the *Titanic* than any other ship, and recent underwater expeditions have ensured that it will never be forgotten. At 46,328 tons, it was the largest vessel afloat, far bigger than its rivals of the Cunard line, the *Lusitania* and the *Mauretania*. It was as long as a football field, with a Turkish bath, gymnasium, swimming pool, squash court, "sidewalk cafes," and elevators. At a top speed of twenty-four to twenty-five knots, it could outstrip almost anything on water.

ABOVE: A joint French-American effort in 1985 located the wreck of the *Titanic,* and, the following year, Dr. Robert D. Ballard of the Woods Hole Oceanographic Institution explored and photographed the remains of the sunken vessel. Despite the passing of more than seventy years, much of the *Titanic* was in amazing condition. This is the window for first class stateroom U on the Boat Deck.

Safety was believed to be paramount. There were sixteen watertight bulkheads but one terrible design flaw—the bulkheads did not reach to the top of the hull, so if one bulkhead was full of water, the water would flow into the neighboring section until the entire hull was full of water. If five adjoining compartments were filled, the ship would begin to sink.

The signs were not auspicious. On April 10, as the *Titanic* was edging out of Southampton to begin her maiden voyage under Captain E. J. Smith, the suction of her huge screws drew the liner *New York* from its moorings and this vessel had to be towed back to the pier, nearly colliding with the *Titanic.* Well on his way across the Atlantic, Captain Smith received iceberg warnings. The weather was clear, at least from

ABOVE: The open forward A-Deck Promenade of the *Titanic,* photographed by Robert Ballard during his 1986 expedition.

the bridge, but not from the crow's nest where the look-out was posted without his binoculars. Speed was not reduced in spite of the warnings—there was a schedule to keep. At 11:40 PM on April 14, the *Titanic* hit an iceberg with a glancing blow. There were sixteen lifeboats and four collapsibles; these could hold only 1,178 of the 2,207 aboard, if all were still functional. Ten miles away the crew of the *Californian* saw the brilliant lights of the *Titanic's* distress rockets, but took no action. The radio operator of the *Titanic* contacted the *Carpathia* fifty-eight miles away, which was "coming hard" at seventeen-and-a-half knots, not her usual speed of fourteen, forcing the boilers almost to breaking point. Unfortunately this was not fast enough, for at 2:20 AM on the morning of the fifteenth the *Titanic* sank, taking over 1,500 people with her.

The rule of "women and children" first was mostly obeyed. The *Carpathia* arrived an hour and ten minutes after the *Titanic* went down. When the *Californian* finally investigated the flares it was much too late to do anything except collect survivors and bodies. There were 705 survivors, and among those who perished were the captain, the designer, and a number of prominent individuals, including the American millionaires John Jacob Astor, Benjamin Guggenheim, and Isidor Straus.

Following this tragedy, safety precautions were revised. Lifeboat drill became compulsory, wireless procedure was altered, and it was declared that in the event of an emergency there would be no more discrimination on grounds of class (steerage-class passengers had been barred from the *Titanic's* boats for a full hour).

The first expedition to locate the wreck of the *Titanic* was a joint French-American effort in 1985. The following year Dr. Robert Ballard of the Woods Hole Oceanographic Institution in Massachusetts explored the remains of the sunken vessel. Though he brought back an extensive photographic record, he decided to leave the wreck undisturbed. However, shortly afterward, a controversial French salvage expedition retrieved dishes, jewels, and currency which were exhibited in Paris in 1987.

World War I

Hardly had the public recovered from the shock of one unsinkable ship going down then there was another disaster. Traveling in dense fog, the *Empress of Ireland* collided with a freighter carrying 10,000 tons of coal on the St. Lawrence river. The *Empress's* bulkheads were designed to be cranked shut by the crew, but they panicked, and the list of the ship was too great to lower all the lifeboats. There were 1,012 casualties and 467 survivors.

World War I made all sea voyages hazardous, though luxury liners appeared to be safe until the sinking of the *Lusitania*. Built in 1907, immensely fast, and able to outdistance any German submarine, the *Lusitania* had crossed the Atlantic 201 times before her fateful voyage from New York to Liverpool in May, 1915. Though the German Embassy had warned Americans not to sail on the boat, there was little concern for personal safety. Lifeboat drill participants numbered only eight men and an officer; none of the other 1,257 passengers paid any attention.

Fog reduced the *Lusitania's* speed to eighteen knots, but the weather cleared, and a warning was sent through that a U-boat was active off the Irish coast. The ship ignored the warning, for it was too close to the coast, and it refused to zigzag, presenting

BELOW: On May 8, 1915, the front page of *The New York Times* announced the loss of the *Lusitania*. It was a tragedy that profoundly shocked the American nation, which had not yet entered the First World War.

THE LOST CUNARD STEAMSHIP LUSITANIA

itself as an easy target. The U-20, which had just sunk two other ships, one without warning, found the easy target, for it misidentified the *Lusitania* as a British auxiliary cruiser and dispatched two torpedoes into its side, causing the ship to list fifteen degrees in a few seconds. There were forty-eight lifeboats—twenty-two wooden, twenty-six collapsible—but lowering them was a shambles, and many collapsed upon each other. Because they had failed to participate in lifeboat drills, a number of passengers put their life jackets on upside down. In all, 1,201 passengers and

ABOVE: The *Lusitania* had crossed the Atlantic 201 times without incident. On May 7th, 1915, she was torpedoed by a German submarine. 1,201 passengers and crew were drowned, including 124 Americans.

crew were drowned, including 124 Americans; 708 were rescued. There is a theory that the ship was carrying munitions because of the massive explosion which occurred when it was struck by the torpedoes.

Most merchant ships were easy prey for U-boats, except for the Q-ships, which appeared to be defenseless but at a moment's notice could reveal themselves as armed merchant cruisers. These U-boats were not the killer-ships of World War II; they were slow and had a limited range but they still caused havoc.

The Royal Navy

An immense reorganization of the Royal Navy took place prior to World War I, thanks to one man, Admiral Sir John Arbuthnot Fisher, first sea lord from 1903 to 1909. Acerbic, controversial, and quarrelsome, Fisher was the toast of ordinary seamen. He improved conditions, made certain that officers were trained, and in hardly more than five years had transformed the Royal Navy from a decrepit array of aged vessels into a great fighting force. He scrapped the old ships without compunction, and brought

BELOW: The sinking of the *Tuscania,* a British transport ship carrying American troops for service in France during World War I, in a 1918 painting by Fred Hoertz. On February 7, 1918, the ship was sunk by a German U-boat off Scotland.

LEFT: The battle of Jutland, May 31 to June 1, 1916, was the only confrontation of the British and German navies during World War I. Although the British lost more ships and men, the German navy returned to port and did not emerge again except to surrender at the war's end. This dramatic picture was painted by Claus Bergen during the actual battle.

FOLLOWING PAGE:
The U-boats of World War I were not the long-range killer ships of World War II. Here, a German U-boat sinks a British fishing vessel in 1917. The crew can be seen rowing to safety. The watercolor was painted during the action by Claus Bergen.

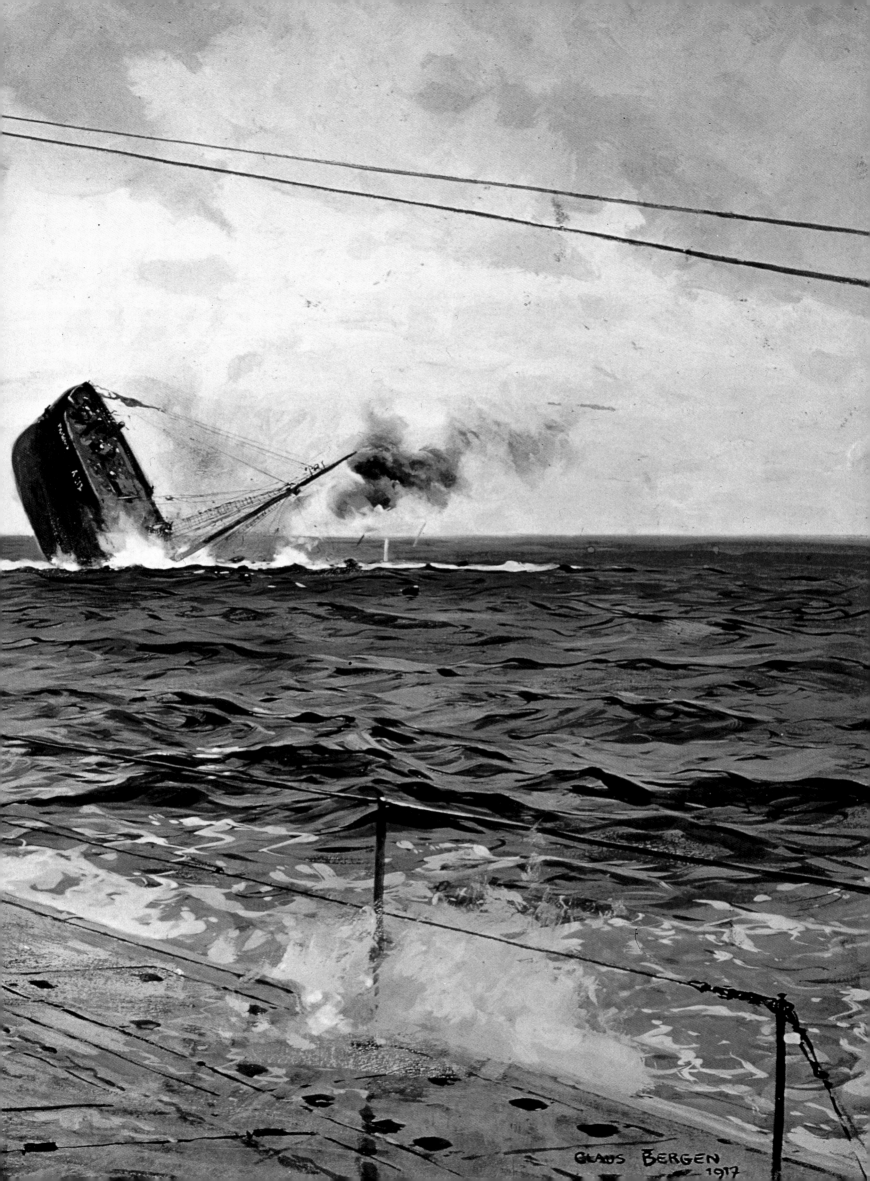

BELOW: Although victorious at Jutland, British battle cruisers were designed as marauders, not as floating batteries, a position they assumed frequently, as is shown in this watercolor by Claus Bergen.

in new combat vessels such as the *Dreadnought*. Like the *Warrior* so many years before, the *Dreadnought* was a world-beater carrying ten twelve-inch guns. She was capable of a speed of twenty to twenty-one knots and used oil turbine propulsion. Fisher also introduced the first battle cruiser, the *Invincible*, with an armament of eight twelve-inch guns and the unheard-of speed of more than twenty-five knots.

Fisher concentrated his main strength in the North Sea and the English Channel, reducing his fleet in the Mediterranean since Germany was clearly going to be the enemy and they did not have access there. He was one of the few men to recognize early on the incredible importance of the submarine. "Good Lord!" he exploded, "if our Admiral is worth his salt, he will tow his submarines at eighteen-knots speed and put

them into the hostile port (like ferrets after the rabbits!) before war is officially declared, just as the Japanese acted before the Russian naval officers knew that war was declared." Politics intervened, and Fisher was forced to resign. If he had remained in his position, he might have altered the course of the First World War through naval power.

As it happened, the only major naval battle in World War I was the Battle of Jutland in May 1916. The outcome was deemed inconclusive; it was claimed as a victory by the British—even though they had more tonnage (a ratio of seven to four) than the Germans. It was a set-piece battle, fought mostly at long range, with at least four to five miles between fleets. Fifteen British admirals flew their pennants in a fleet consisting of twenty-eight dreadnoughts, nine battle cruisers, nine cruisers, twenty-two light cruisers, and eighty-two destroyers. There were forty more destroyers available, but

because of a breakdown of communications they were not present. The British lost twice as many men as the Germans— 6,787 to 3,039. The battle cruisers were vulnerable; they had not been used as Fisher had wanted—as fast marauders— but it was the Germans who gave way in the end. At the conclusion of the war the German fleet surrendered, made its way to the naval base at Scapa Flow in the Shetland Islands off Scotland, and scuttled itself.

Between the Wars

Between the two world wars there were fewer great sea disasters. One of these was the *Vestris*, en route to Buenos Aires from New York with 128 passengers and 6,000 tons of cargo. Even before she set out, acute observers noticed that the ship was listing slightly. No one knew that she already had a number of leaks. After a severe storm, the vessel was listing twenty degrees, and three cars in the cargo hold thundered through the bulkheads. The captain remained confident. He did not send out an SOS or decrease his speed. When a passenger complained of water coming through his porthole, a steward explained that it was only a

minor leak. By the time the ship was listing thirty degrees, the passengers were very alarmed. Usable lifeboats were, as always, in short supply. The ship sank suddenly. Out of the 325 who sailed, 110 were lost. None of the children and only a few women survived.

One of the oddest shipwrecks occurred in 1923 in thick fog off San Miguel Island, California, when the steamship *Cuba* ran aground. Eighteen US Navy ships were in the vicinity on maneuvers, and they all came to help, literally piling up one upon the other. Of the 652 seamen involved, twenty-two died. There was a court of inquiry, but it was never published.

In February 1939, a small British freighter named the *Lutzen* was on her way from St. John's, New Brunswick, to New York with 230 tons of frozen blueberries when she went aground. Local people helped to unload, but they took all the cargo from the starboard side, so that when the next tide came in, it tipped the ship over on its port side and the salvage operation had to be abandoned.

There were near disasters. The *Egypt*, a huge ship of the Pacific and Orient line, was rammed and sunk in the Bay of Biscay in 1922. The vessel was designed to carry five hundred passengers, but there were only forty-four aboard since it was considered a social error to board a P. and O. liner in Britain. The proper thing to do was to travel by train to Dover, cross the channel to France, travel by train to Marseilles, and pick up the ship there. Not only was loss of life averted, but more than a million pounds in gold carried by the *Egypt* was later recovered.

World War II

Merchant ship losses were horrendous during World War II. The first merchant ship to be dispatched to the bottom was the *Athenia* on September 4, 1939, the second day of the war. Ships could be replaced, but not the seamen; they stood a one-in-four chance of being drowned, and lived and worked under atrocious conditions. In some ships space was so limited that men had to stand up to eat and took turns sleeping in whatever hammocks were available. So many ships were sunk that a catalog would be meaningless, and there was no single tragedy, such as the *Lusitania*, for the world to focus upon.

The convoy system helped to minimize losses, especially when long-range aircraft could cover most of the route from America and to Britain. At least 2,200 convoys with a total of 75,000 merchant ships crossed the Atlantic. These were often protected by American naval forces and the destroyers provided to Britain under the Lease-Lend

ABOVE: In this combat photograph, the first ever taken through a periscope, a Japanese destroyer sinks after being torpedoed by an American submarine on July 25, 1942.

LEFT: The ship's telegraph of the *Shinkoku Maru*, one of the Japanese warships sunk in Truk Lagoon, where the wrecks remain untouched, as the Philippine government has banned salvage and bounty hunters.

RIGHT: The wrecks of many Japanese ships from World War II are easily observed in the clear waters of Truk Lagoon.

ABOVE: "Battleship Row" in Pearl Harbor, Hawaii, can easily be spotted in this aerial photograph taken from a Japanese airplane during the attack on December 7, 1941.

Act of 1941, before the United States entered the war. U-boat losses were heavy—at least eight hundred. Neutral ships were fair game and many went to the bottom, even "neutrals" who were aiding the Germans.

There were great naval tragedies. Soon after war was declared the British vessel *Royal Oak* was sunk in the harbor at Scapa Flow by a German U-boat that managed to penetrate the protecting boom. More than eight hundred men died when it sank in seconds. The *Prince of Wales* and the *Repulse* were lost with tremendous casualties, sunk by Japanese aircraft off Malaysia. These losses damaged morale and made the capture of Singapore inevitable. HMS *Hood*, a 42,100-ton antique battle cruiser built between 1918 and 1920, was an easy victim. The formidable German battleship *Bismarck* gave its pursuers a run for their money, and was sunk only by a combination of luck, naval guns, and airborne torpedoes. The pocket battleship *Graf Spee* was harassed and savaged by lighter-armed British cruisers early in the war in the South Atlantic, and the captain scuttled his ship in the harbor at Montevideo, Uruguay, before committing suicide.

Many warships were sunk on mundane duties while acting as escorts; others were mined, or sunk by land-based artillery while bombarding enemy positions.

Pearl Harbor

The first catastrophe to be fully covered by newsreel was the surprise Japanese attack on the US naval base at Pearl Harbor, Hawaii, which demonstrated the vulnerability of ships to carrier-borne aircraft. On December 7, 1941, in an act of aggression that came before a formal declaration of war, the Japanese successfully repeated tactics from the Russo-Japanese war forty years earlier. Nineteen American vessels were

RIGHT: Japanese ships set ablaze by American Operation Hailstone, February, 1944, in Truk Lagoon, an important Japanese naval base in the Phillipines.

RIGHT: During the Japanese attack on Pearl Harbor, the battleship *Arizona* sank within nine minutes of being bombed. 1,177 men of a crew of 1,500 died. The *Arizona* remains in forty feet of water, the centerpiece of a national memorial visited by 1.5 million people each year.

LEFT: The most-dived wreck at Truk Lagoon is the *Fujikawa Maru.* As these wrecks lie at a reasonable depth, they can be explored without using sophisticated equipment.

LEFT: Among the items found by divers in Truk Lagoon are reminders of everyday life, such as these shoes discovered in the wreck of the *Kiyosumi Maru.*

LEFT: Many of the visible items at Truk Lagoon are enigmatic and mysterious, which often adds to the enjoyment of divers who have to puzzle out what they are.

destroyed or badly damaged in the attack, including eight bat-tleships—the *Arizona, Oklahoma, California, Maryland, Pennsylvania, Tennessee, Nevada*, and the *West Virginia*—which had been moored in what was known as Battleship Row. About three thousand naval and military personnel were killed or wounded, and nearly two hundred American aircraft were destroyed, mostly on the ground. On December 8, 1941, the United States declared war on Japan.

Truk Lagoon

In 1944, at Truk Lagoon in the Philippines, the Americans launched a devastating attack by carrier-borne aircraft on the Japanese fleet. A large number of wrecks remain untouched there, and the Philippine government has banned salvage and bounty hunting. Over one hundred wrecks have been charted, and there would have been more had not a large part of the Japanese fleet departed before the raid. Some of the cargo is virtually intact, including the once-notorious Zero fighter planes. The most-dived wreck at Truk Lagoon is probably the *Fujikawa Maru*, where the guns date back to the Russo-Japanese war. The *Aikoku Maru* is also attractive to divers, although she lies at a far greater depth.

ABOVE: Below deck on the wreck of the *Sankisan Maru*, another of the wrecked Japanese battleships entombed beneath the waters of Truk Lagoon.

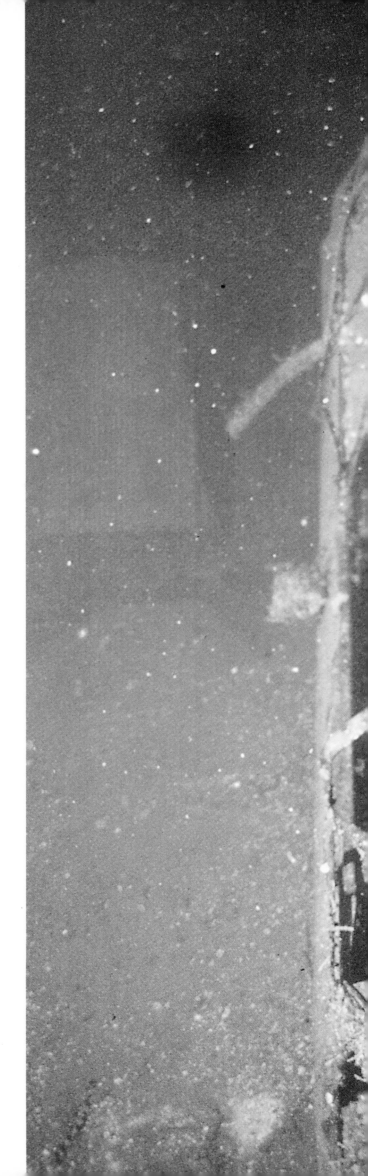

RIGHT: The cockpit of a fighter plane in the bottom hold of the *Fujikawa Maru* at Truk Lagoon. The ship was carrying the notorious Zero fighter planes, some of which are nearly intact.

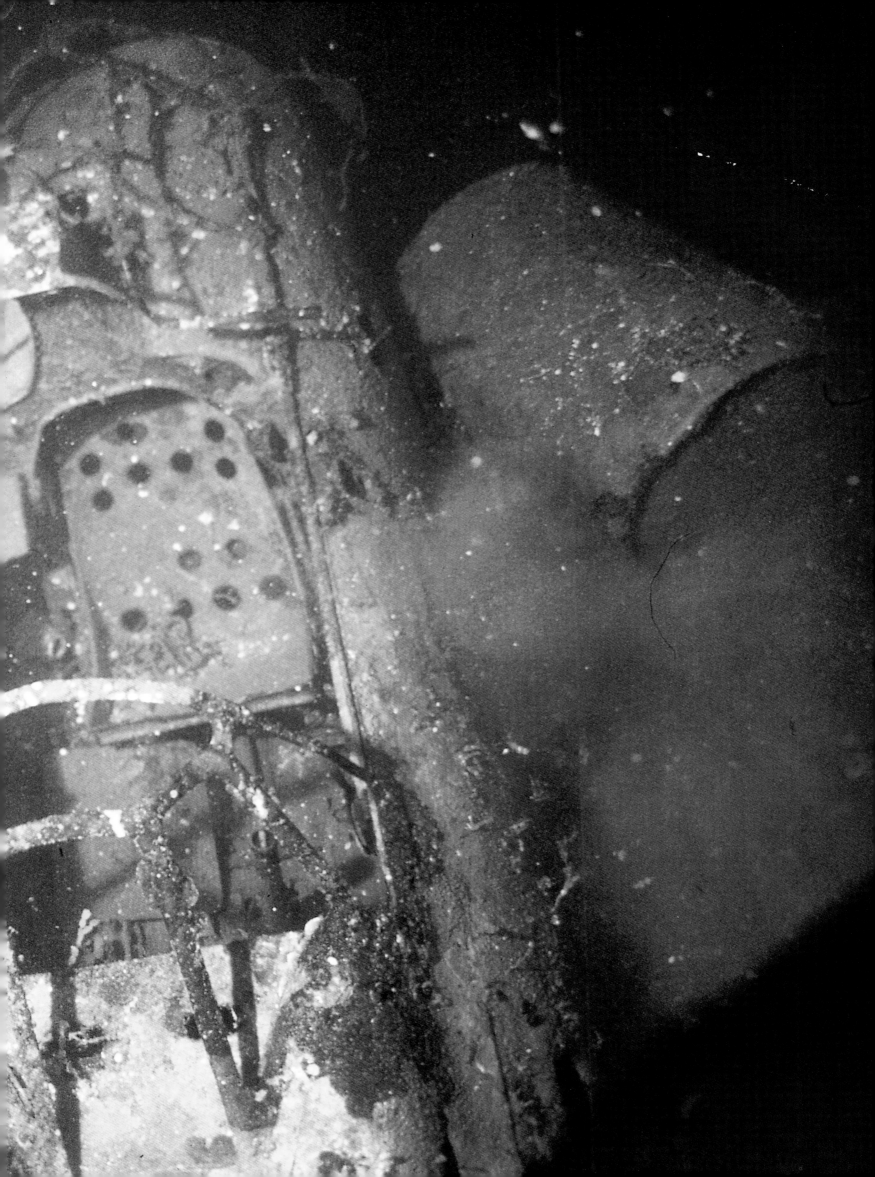

Radar

There were tremendous changes at sea after World War II. Radar made collisions rarer, but within the space of a generation the ocean passenger liner was practically obsolete, rendered out-of-date almost overnight because of the boom in air travel. Yet sea travel today has revived modestly because of the increasing popularity of vacation cruises.

Though the sinking of the *Titanic* could not happen now, we should consider the lesson of the *Andrea Doria*, an Italian ship completed in 1951 and launched on its maiden voyage in 1953. This 29,100-ton vessel was luxuriously equipped and capable of twenty-three knots, but, like the *Titanic*, her bulkheads did not extend to the deck. On her way across the Atlantic in 1956 the *Andrea Doria* encounted fog, but having radar meant that any

FOLLOWING PAGE:
Instant communications by radio and satellite now bring immediate help to most unexpected accidents. This fire aboard the Norwegian vessel *Megaborg* was quickly extinguished.

LEFT: Many vessels in the shallow Gulf of Suez were either sunk by an enemy during a war or deliberately scuttled to inhibit navigation and impede the transportation of oil and other vital commodities.

dangerous icebergs could be detected at a safe distance and avoided. Because of a tight schedule—passengers became irritable if they missed their train, bus, or plane connections in the United States—the captain lowered his speed only slightly. When a pip was detected on the radar it was assumed to be a small fishing vessel, and the captain decided that it would be safe to pass. He was wrong. The *Andrea Doria* collided with the 12,165-ton *Stockholm*, which had also plotted the *Andrea Doria* on radar.

The *Andrea Doria* began quickly to list, and there was no doubt that it would sink. Many ships in the neighborhood came to help with the rescue, including the *Stockholm*, which although damaged could still function. (The *Stockholm* nearly hit the *Andrea Doria* again, however, because its sea anchor had moored the vessel to the bottom.) Fifty-one people died, and it was noticed that the first people in the boats were the crew. The inquiry afterwards could not explain why the accident had happened, but then radar was not magic, and assumption had taken the place of fact checking.

The postwar years also saw the development of the oil tanker and other bulk container ships. The *Torrey Canyon*, which went aground off the Scilly Islands in March 1967, causing tremendous pollution, weighed 123,000 tons. She was trying to take a shortcut to catch the tide at Milford Haven, in Wales. To avoid further pollution, the *Torrey Canyon* was bombed from the air and set on fire.

FAR LEFT: The stories behind many visible shipwrecks have been obscured by time. This cargo vessel, lost at Tiladummati Atoll in the Maldives, may well have been caught up in a typhoon.

RIGHT: Even in modern times, safety is not guaranteed. Fire sweeps through the *Queen Elizabeth* in 1972 in Hong Kong.

RIGHT: The wreck of the Queen Elizabeth sinks into the sea after the terrible fire has run its course.

RIGHT: The rocky shores of many nations have become infamous as ships' graveyards. This spot along the Irish coast has claimed a freighter which will be eventually broken up by the action of wind and waves.

The *Marpessa,* which went down in 1969, weighed 207,000 tons. The *Exxon Valdez,* a tanker stranded on Bligh Reef in 1989, spilled almost a quarter of a million tons of crude oil into the untroubled waters of Alaska, yet it ranked only tenth in capacity on a world-wide scale. The crew numbered twenty men, and though the ship was mostly on autopilot, careful steering by hand was necessary in confined waters such as those at Bligh Reef. The captain was known to like his drink, and in the investigation following the disaster it was discovered that he had been convicted twice for drunken driving. Some of the crew were found to be at fault as well.

This is a scenario which is not unique—it is, in fact, all too familiar. "Human error" is part of the human condition. Radar, computer technology, and satellite navigation are all tools to be applied purposefully; they cannot be used like magic. Mistakes at sea in the 1990s can still spread catastrophe, as can that perennial cause of disaster—human greed.

LEFT: The tanker *Exxon Valdez* spilled almost a quarter of a million tons of crude oil into the untroubled waters of Alaska in 1989. Here, the *Exxon Valdez* offloads some of its remaining cargo of oil to another tanker.

ABOVE: One morning in 1984, a woman in Palm Beach, Florida, found a tramp steamer practically in her swimming pool—it had been blown ashore during the night. The ship was successfully refloated and the pool was found to be undamaged.

AFTERWORD

The overriding question concerning shipwrecks is a moral one. Is it *right* to disturb a wreck—especially if it is, ultimately, a mass grave?

Some wrecks have had proscriptions put on them. The *Royal Oak,* for example, has been designated a war grave, and diving on her is strictly prohibited by law even though it is one of the most intact wrecks in the northern hemisphere. The battleship *Arizona,* which lies at rest beneath the waters at Pearl Harbor, is similarly protected.

In addition, Japanese ships sunk in Truk Lagoon have been put off-limits by the Philippine government. But many wrecks in clear water, such as those around Bermuda and off the east coast of Australia, have become tourist attractions, and tales of millions of dollars worth of gold bullion, whether true or fictitious, are enough to spark frantic and well-funded expeditions.

As for the merits of marine archaeology, is there anything more to be learned from the artifacts recovered from sunken ships? Almost certainly. The contents of no two wrecks are the same, making each vessel a time capsule which can and will increase our knowledge of the past if recovered.

Deep-sea exploration becomes easier every year, and increasingly sophisticated technology, from miniature submarines to remote-controlled robots and cameras, means that perhaps no wreck, even one hidden in the deepest crevices of the ocean, is ultimately unreachable. The investigation of the *Titanic,* at two-and-a-half miles deep, may be seen as a turning point in deep-sea exploration.

The ocean depths are the last great wildernesses yet to be thoroughly explored. They are also graveyards for hundreds of thousands of ships. Most of those within easy reach have been pillaged, but there will always be the belief that the next wreck to be discovered may contain treasure beyond one's wildest dreams—and perhaps clues and information long lost to history, which are in the end more valuable than gold.

RIGHT: Modern technology has made it easy to document underwater wrecks both old and new. Here, the wreck of the *Eagle* in the Florida Keys has been recorded for posterity.

INDEX